AF540262

Meditation

The Awakening of Inner Powers

Meditation

The Awakening of Inner Powers

Swami Bodhananda

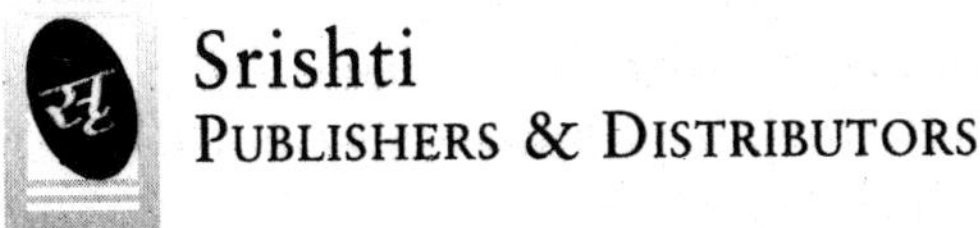
Srishti
Publishers & Distributors

SRISHTI PUBLISHERS & DISTRIBUTORS
N-16, C. R. Park
New Delhi 110 019
srishtipublishers@gmail.com

Copyright © Sambodh Foundation

First published by Sambodh Foundation 1995

First published by Srishti Publishers & Distributors 2003

This impression 2011

Cover lithograph: Nirmal Parkash

Inside photograph & illustration: Sambodh Foundation

Cover design by Creative Concept

Typeset in AGaramond 11pt. Skumar at Srishti

This edition is only for sale in India, Pakistan, Bangladesh and Nepal.

All rights reserved. No part of this publication may be reproduced, stored in a retrieval system, or transmitted, in any form or by any means, electronic, mechanical, photocopying, recording or otherwise, without the prior written permission of the Publishers.

Contents

Acknowledgements

Meditation: the Awakening of Inner Powers was first transcribed from a series of talks I gave in Ernakulum, Kerala. Dr. Sangeetha Menon was responsible for this task as well as for editing the first edition of this book. Without her singular devotion to those initial efforts this most recent project could not have been completed.

Ganesha on the cover is an interpretation of The Sambodh Foundation symbol inspired at the time our organizations were first formulated in India. As our organization spread from India to America, The Sambodh Society, Inc. adopted this same symbol for our organizations forming there. Erika Jackson kindly contributed the artwork for both the illustrations of the *mudras* given in Chapter 2 as well as the original cover design.

We began thinking about a revised edition for an American audience during my first visit to the United States in 1997. At that time I was in Kalamazoo, Michigan, staying with Drs. Richard and Ruth Harring. We began with the time-consuming task of creating a glossary of Sanskrit terms for a western audience. In this glossary, I have given my own definitions suited to the particular purpose of this work. I am very grateful to Dr. Ruth Harring for her meticulous editing of the second edition for western readers and devotees, her painstaking development of the new components, as well as for coordinating the various aspects necessary to bring out the 2001 edition.

I thank all who contributed, directly or indirectly, to its production.

Now I thank Srishti Publishers for bringing out this edition for the subcontient. The glossary has been retained for the westernised reader who may not be familiar with a basic Vedantic vocabulary or who may wish to have a deeper understanding. To this end some useful slokas have been included in the appendix with an English translation, and Sri Sankaracharya's injuctions for the sincere seeker.

The book is conceived more as a heart-oriented and experiential approach to meditation, than head-oriented and logical. Since it was first presented as a series of sessions in Ernakulum, Kerala, for a "live" audience interested in meditation, its 'live' character has been retained. You will be *hearing* it, rather than *reading*. Read until you complete the text. Then choose the meditation you would like to try. Go slowly and practise everyday. The Sanskrit *slokas* and quotations are, at times, left untranslated within the text in order to heighten your experience of reading. I suggest that you keep a diary of all the words and *slokas* whose meanings you don't quite grasp. Read again. Meanwhile, so much will have happened around you and within you, elevating the entire journey into a cosmic flowering. After the seventh reading, the total experience of the meaning will descend upon you as a Divine gift.

19 October, 2002 Swami Bodhananda

New Delhi

Sankaracharya's Forty Steps to God Realization

The great *Advaita Guru* and Saint,
Poojya Pada Sankaracharya, (788-820 AD)
wrote some lines of advice for the benefit of
sincere seekers after Truth –
for those who pine for God.

Swami Bodhananda renders his priceless verses
from Sanskrit into an idiom intelligible
to modern seekers who are looking
for values to enrich their lives and are groping
for visions to experience the living
presence of God in their daily existence.

1. *Study the Vedas daily.*
2. *Lovingly perform duties enjoined by the Vedas.*
3. *Perform your duties as an offering to the Lord, as worship unto Him.*
4. *Renounce desire-prompted, selfish activities.*
5. *Clean up the mind-stream of all sins; save the mind from likes, dislikes and reactions.*
6. *Recognize the limitations of worldly pleasures.*
7. *Cultivate love for the Self.*
8. *Leave behind all binding attachments.*
9. *Associate with good people.*
10. *Develop deep devotion to God.*
11. *Be of a pleasant and peaceful disposition.*
12. *Take refuge at the lotus feet of an Enlightened Master.*
13. *Daily serve the Guru, worshipping His feet.*
14. *Seek instructions on the mystic meaning of* Om *the* Pranava, *the symbol of* Brahman, *the Immutable One.*
15. *Listen to expositions on the* Upanishad's *revelations, the crown of Scriptures.*
16. *Reflect upon the significance and meaning of scriptural statements.*
17. *Lovingly follow the line of thought revealed in the* Upanishads.
18. *Avoid fruitless discussion and bad logic.*

19. *Let your reasoning process resonate with the thought-rhythm of the* Upaniṣhads.
20. *Deeply feel the throb of* Brahman *in the depth of your soul: "I am Brahman, the Supreme Bliss."*
21. *Shun ignorance in moment-to-moment interactions and personal relationships.*
22. *Give up body identification.*
23. *Avoid self-opinionated arguments with wise persons.*
24. *Get treated in hunger and disease.*
25. *Eat food as a medicine.*
26. *Don't crave for tasty food, titillating to the palate.*
27. *Be content with food that comes God-sent.*
28. *Endure the inevitable polarities, the pairs of opposites, in life situations – e.g. heat-cold and pain-pleasure.*
29. *Avoid the dissipation of energy in fruitless discussions and idle talk.*
30. *Be ever vigilant, alert and detached.*
31. *Avoid reacting to praise and criticism.*
32. *Live happily in solitude; enjoy aloneness.*
33. *Abide in the Oceanic Consciousness; Realize the fullness of Self.*
34. *Experience the world of sensations as a manifestation of that Self.*
35. *See the absence of a separate world in that all-enveloping Bliss.*

36. *Dissolve the entire conditioning of the past.*

37. *Ignore all those bitter memories and their influence on the present.*

38. *With the power of wisdom, remain free from idle hopes and expectations.*

39. *Don't be disheartened and dismayed by the pressures of present challenges.*

40. *Make your weaknesses into strengths and your adversities into opportunities.*

    Thus, live in the eternal Bliss of Brahman, *totally immersed in God-Consciousness.*

An Overview

What is Meditation?

Meditation is abiding in the Self as a totally happy person. Dynamic meditation is abiding in the Self while interacting with the world. Planning and working for maximum success in the world can be, in itself, a deep experience of meditation.

Why Techniques?

In the beginning, the meditator needs the help of techniques to master the ultimate meditation. The controlled conditions of a swimming pool are necessary for a novice learning to swim. The turbulence of the world and incessant storms in the mind impede the self-awareness necessary for meditation, and techniques help overcome these impediments.

How does One Stabilize the Mind?

The *prana* plays a vital role in the activity of the mind. *Prana* is the vital energy that governs all voluntary and involuntary activities of the individual. Breathing is the grossest expression of *prana,* and we all know that the individual cannot survive without breath. *Prana* is at the root of all psychological, physiological and physical functions. Therefore, by controlling *prana,* by exercising breath control, the whole mind-body complex can be brought into a new level of efficiency and creative health. This, in turn, creates a conducive state of mind for meditation.

Why are Physical Postures Important?

The right posture of the physical body helps in activating *prana* and in organizing the thought processes. One who stands erect, with his head high and chest up, experiences a higher level of energy than one who slouches with his head down and body shifting about. The ancient *rishis* of India devised various physical postures for activating the various energy centres of the human body and for unleashing the free flow of *prana* though all the nerve channels. These postures are called *asanas* and *mudras*.

Which *Asana* is Conducive for Meditation?

Sthirasukhamasanam – any steady and comfortable posture in which one can sit for 45 minutes is considered a good posture for meditation. However, the posture generally recommended is called *sukhasana*, that is, to sit cross-legged with your hands resting on the knees, your eyes effortlessly closed, your attention focused upon on the *bhrumadhya,* the point between the eyebrows, and observing the *prana*, the in-going and out-going breath.

What are Mudras, and How do They Affect *Prana* and Mind?

Mudras are hand gestures performed deliberately – or that sometimes arise spontaneously – during meditation. Some of the *mudras* discussed in this book are as follows: *sukha, jnana, dhyana, yoga, bhakti, saranagati, prapatti, bodha, prasada* and *ananda.* (Please see the diagrams provided in Chapter 2.) *Mudras* help activate the *cakras* and lift the life energy from the primeval limitations of anger, desire and greed to a more expansive awareness of compassion, austerity and sharing. These gestures are capable of launching the seeker into the land of a thousands lotuses in full bloom, the ultimate state of meditation.

What is *Pranayama*?

Pranayama is regulating the process of breathing. It includes: *puraka* – deep, slow inhaling; *antakumbhaka* – retaining the inhaled breath; *recaka* – slow controlled exhaling; and, *bahyakumbhaka* – retaining breath outside and keeping the lungs empty. Through the practice of *pranayama* one is able to activate the flow of vital energy (the *prana*) and streamline the metabolic activities, like ingestion, digestion, circulation, assimilation and excretion, enhancing the overall condition of the mind-body. The details of *pranayama* are to be learned directly from a *Guru*.

What is the Importance of Chanting *Mantras* in Meditation?

The meditator has to be initiated by a *siddha guru* into *mantra*, and the *diksha mantra* has to be held as a secret in one's heart during the course of *sadhana*. *Mantra* becomes powerless when exposed, just as a seed taken out of the soil is powerless to sprout and grow.

Sound is an instrument by which *prana* can be activated, opening the energy centres and organizing the mind for mediation. *Mantra* is a string of potential sounds to be chanted by which one cleans the thought-stream, unleashing fresh energy from within.

Does Visualization Help in Integrating the Mind?

Positive visualization – either of the unity and integrity of diverse phenomena, or of the inspiring faces of Mother Nature like a lotus flower, or of the adorable form of gods, such as Krishna or Rama, and of the Supreme Lord – is helpful in integrating the mind for meditation. Any of the above visualizations revitalize the *prana* and uplift the mind.

Chanting *mantras* helps the individual energy centres – *cakras* and *indriyas* – resonate with the cosmic energy centres known as *devatas.* Visualization of and concentration upon the *devatas* help to create positive thought currents capable of drawing *anugraha*, energy and inspiration, from the *devatas.*

What is the Role of Witnessing and Silence in Meditation?

Finally, it is pure witnessing and the power of silence that consumes the ego centre and lifts the meditator to the dimension of peace and supreme creative bliss, a state of *total* Self-abidance.

Dynamic Meditation

Human beings have three types of activities, *viz.* physical, mental and spiritual. Everybody knows about physical activities, like lifting your hands, moving your legs, walking, sitting, etc. Apart from the physical activities there are mental activities like thinking, reflecting, being silent, gathering poise, etc. Mental activities create ideas and thoughts that change and fashion the world. Beyond physical and mental activity is the highest activity – a spiritual activity that we call meditation.

To begin with, meditation is also an activity. Let us call it a spiritual activity. This spiritual activity, which is meditation, is the highest vocation in life. It requires a very subtle mind. A gross mind may enjoy gross activities, but it is only a subtle mind that enjoys reflection, thought and meditation. Mind can be divided into three states – the gross, the sharp and the subtle. A sharp mind – *tikshna buddhi* – is good at thinking, planning and analyzing. It is a scientist's mind. This type of mind can cut through the complex web of matter and discover the physical laws underlying this chaotic world. As mind further evolves, it becomes more subtle – *sukshma buddhi* – a meditative mind.

The meditative mind is the highest state of mind. Meditation is an activity higher than thought. We have physical, mental and spiritual activities, and through the activities of meditation we understand the oneness of existence that is God. To realize God as the oneness of existence, we have to meditate. One has to think in order to understand the logic and structure of the universe of matter. To change the world according to our needs and convenience, we have to act. All these types of activities are important in their own realms. One should not occur at the cost of another. Meditation should not be done at the cost of thinking; thinking should not be done at the cost of other activities. In fact, they are all mutually reinforcing. It is only a very active person who can think. It is only a very thoughtful person who can meditate. Let us not presume, "I am a meditator, therefore, I don't think or act." One cannot meditate without performing other activities; nor can one act *without* meditation. Any activity without its complement, meditation, becomes very shallow. It lacks the power of the spirit, and one doesn't enjoy such an activity.

The general notion that activity is opposed to meditation, and that meditation is opposed to thinking, is a false notion. That is why we schedule the practice of meditation for the evening – we know that at that time our minds will be very agitated, upset with all our problems. We should meditate in the thick of problems. If a *rishi* can stand on the tip of a needle and meditate, why can't we meditate in the midst of all this "mental" noise? Meditation is to be practiced in the *midst* of the din and roar of the battlefield.

We are presenting meditation in such a way that is not opposed to activity, that is not opposed to thought, but on the contrary, will become a nourishment to our thinking and our activities. Activities become nourishment for meditation; they infuse energy into one another and create a wholeness of experience.

In *Sanatana-dharma*, God means "the wholeness of things." The more we integrate things, the more divinity manifests in us. When we sit together, there is a greater manifestation of divinity. When you place more and more things in the ambience of your consciousness, more and more divinity manifests. That is how we eventually come to appreciate and understand God. God is the togetherness of things. God need not be a particular person. Of course, one can invoke God as a person. Sankara gives six ways of invoking God known as the *Sadmata Sampradaya.* *"Mata"* means a "method," a way, a way of invoking divinity. One can invoke divinity in six ways, or by six methods, or in six forms. The *Saureyas* invoke God in the form of *Surya* through *Surya upasana.* Those who invoke God in the form of *Ganesh* are known as *Ganapatyas.* The *Kaumaras* invoke God in the form of *Kumara.* The *Vaisnavas* invoke God in the form of *Vishnu.* The *Sakteyas* invoke God in the form of *Sakti.* The *Saivas* invoke God in the form of *Siva.* These constitute the six forms Sankara mentions as methods of invoking God.

Those who wear *rudraksa mala* and *vibhuti* are generally *Saivas.* Those who wear crystal *mala* and vermilion are *Sakteyas.* And those who wear *tulsi mala* and sandal paste are *Vaisnavas.*

The meditator need not be concerned with the form of God. We believe that God can take any form. Meditation is an activity we undertake to experience the divinity in everything. It is a state of mind. One must be able to see the divinity in every manifestation of existence, experience the universe integrally. Generally, we think that meditation is something like focusing on the tip of a flame. When you focus on the tip of the flame – *trataka* – of course you gain concentration, but you may also get a headache! Concentration is only an initial step of meditation. The highest state of meditation (which will be expounded upon later) is experiencing the whole universe integrally. The universe is made up of various parts, just as one's body is made up of various parts – head, trunk, neck, hand, leg, toes, etc. Each of these again has various parts, but how do you experience them? How do you experience your nose? As part of your whole system! The physical body is one integral, organic system not merely discrete parts. Just as I experience every limb in me integrally, I don't say, "My nose is nearer to me than the toe," or "My toe is far away. Do anything to my toe, but don't touch my nose or I will get angry." This kind of difference is not there. Whether it is the nose or toe, these are all parts of our whole body. We experience them integrally.

Differences are not opposed to the integral experience of things. Differences are there. Parts are there. Difference is *not* division. We can all be different, unique individuals. Still, we all share a common existence. That common existence which we share, of which we are integral parts and limbs, is God.

Human consciousness can experience that integrality of existence that Aurobindo calls "Integral Yoga." When you become an integrated person, then the whole of existence can be experienced integrally. This is the idea of meditation: it is other than thinking; it is other than activity. It nourishes one's thinking and activity; it is experiencing everything integrally. Ultimately, it is a state of total love for everything in the universe. One is in love with the universe. When we are in love with the universe, we can say that we are in meditation. It is an experience of the continuous explosion of energies within one's self. You feel that energy streaming forth in all your activities. This is how we understand meditation, and that is why we refer to this meditation as *Dynamic Meditation.*

Siva is in meditation while He dances. Christ suffering on the cross was in meditation. Ramana Maharshi, with the cancerous wound, was in meditation. Pain and activity did not affect the quality and purity of their consciousness, though, from the outside world, they all appeared to be suffering. They were not suffering; they all *appeared* to be suffering. They were not suffering; they were in meditation. This is how we can begin to understand meditation in the midst of activities.

The instrument of meditation is the mind. So what is mind? Mind is that which mediates between Consciousness and the world. One can say that mind acts as a bridge between Consciousness and the world. There is a world around us. We are experiencing the world as a set of discrete objects. We are conscious of all this. We are conscious beings. If anybody has any doubt about his being conscious, one may inquire, "Are you conscious of that doubt?" Therefore, we may realize, without any doubt, that we are all conscious beings. Consciousness is self-evident; no proof is necessary. Do I require proof of my own existence – for my being conscious? If I say, "I doubt my being conscious," I have made a self-contradictory statement. It is something like shouting, "I am a dumb person." A dumb person cannot shout! To say that I doubt my being conscious is a contradiction. Consciousness is self-evident; it requires no proof.

One's claim must originate upon some ground which does not require any proof. If the statement itself requires proof, then it is not a profound statement. For example, when someone asks, "Where is Australia?" and you answer, "Australia is near New Zealand." And, conversely, to the question, "Where is New Zealand?" you answer, "New Zealand is near Australia." This kind of response reveals no understanding; it goes round and round. So, can we start from somewhere that does not require any proof, which does not require any other statement to support it? The point that is self-evident, about which we don't require any proof, is our own existence or Consciousness – "I am a conscious being." It is something about which I can have no doubt whatsoever. Thus, Consciousness, through the mind, experiences the entire world. That is why I said that mind is an instrument that mediates between Consciousness – which is self-evident – and the world, about whose existence we have no knowledge except that we are experiencing it. We neither know from where it has come, nor why it has come, nor how long it has existed.

Now, it is clear that there are three categories: Consciousness, the world, and then the mind – the joining link mediating between the first two. Consciousness, shining upon the mind, is the soul. When you say "I," which is that I? It is Consciousness falling upon the mind. You are conscious of the mind. You know that you have a mind – good, bad or indifferent. Consciousness falling upon the mind is the soul that I am today, the individual. We are all individuals. Consciousness falls upon the mind just as sunlight falls upon the moon. The moon has no light of its own. In Vedanta the mind is compared to the moon. The moon is an entity that borrows light from the sun and is supposed to be the *devata* of mind. That is why on a full moon day mad people become more deranged, and people, in general, become more excited. Oceans heave high on the full moon day. Animals run hither and thither in the forest, because much excitement is aroused on the full moon day. On the new moon day, when there is no visible moon, everyone is sleepy. Then *tamas* is greater.

A connection exists between the cosmos and the individual mind, though an ordinary person is not able to inter-link these properly nor identify the connections. Our *rishis* discovered these connections and connected every sense organ with its complementary star. The human mind cannot scientifically explore and explain those connections, though we have made partially successful efforts.

When Consciousness falls upon the mind, just as sunlight falls upon the moon, the mind becomes a shining entity, a conscious entity. It is that reflected light of Consciousness in the mind which shoots through the sense organs. Whatever falls in the path of that reflected light, shooting through the sense organs, is related to our consciousness. Then there exist the "I," "he" and "this" – the self, the other, and the objects of creation. Sankara gives a beautiful illustration in *Dakshinamurti Stotram*:

Nanacchidraghadodarasthiha maha
dipaprabha bhasvaram
Jnanam yasya tu caksuradikarana
dvara bahihspandate,
Janamiti tameva bhantamanubha –
tyetatsamastam jagat
Tasmai Sri Guru murtaye nama idam Sri Dakshinamurtaye.

(Hymn to *Dakshinamurti*, *sloka* iv)

Sankara says that we are like a rounded pot with five apertures on its "belly." A lamp is inside the pot that fills the pot with light. First the flame fills the pot with light. Then the light shoots out through the apertures in the belly of the pot, casting trajectories of light. Whatever falls in those trajectories is illuminated. Haven't you sometimes seen the bright sunlight beaming through a small opening? Whatever falls in the path of the light becomes vibrant; all the dust particles dance and become alive. This same way, Consciousness first fills us inside, and then it shoots through the five apertures. The five apertures are the ear, nose, tongue, eyes and skin. Through these sense organs the reflected consciousness shoots out. And whatever falls in that light is illuminated: sound, smell, taste, form and touch – everything is illuminated – and that is our existence.

The structure of existence needs to be understood, otherwise one will not be able to meditate. Someone said, "I meditate everyday." I asked in return, "What are you meditating upon?" "That my *Guru* alone knows; he told me to meditate everyday," was his reply. But, unless we know the very structure of existence – who is meditating, what is meditated upon, and what is the instrument of meditation – meditation is not possible. Mind is the instrument of meditation that mediates between Consciousness and the world. Consciousness falling upon the mind, reflecting in the mind is the *jiva*. It is reflected consciousness that illumines the world and knows the world. After all, what is living but a parade of cognition, a stream of cognition? Early in the morning when we wake up we start cognizing – "I see, I touch, I smell." This is the parade of cognition. Consciousness is that which illumines the world and mind – the *jivatman* is that which lights up the experiencer who experiences the world.

The mind, all the time, seeks. It seeks outside. The mind seeking outside is an ignorant mind. Generally, the mind is all the time extroverted:

Paranci khani vyatrnat svayambhuh
tasmat paran pasyati na antaratman
kaschit dhirah pratyagatmanam aikshat
Avrtta caksur amrtatvam icchan

(*Kathopanishad*, II.iv.i)

As of today, we are extroverted. We are always moving outside, not physically but mentally. You are here physically, but where are you mentally? All the time, we are thinking about a million and one things. This mental meandering into futile pursuits is our state of mind today. That is why we experience dissipation, why we have no energy. We are totally exhausted – without doing anything!

So, what is the mind seeking? Above all, the mind seeks happiness. Happiness is the object that the mind seeks from the world outside. Such a mind is known as an *ignorant* mind. Why is it ignorant? Because it ignores the happiness it *is* and seeks happiness outside itself. The noun "ignorance" is born of the verb "ignore." What is the mind ignoring? Mind ignores the fact that it is sitting on a treasure chest of happiness. That is why the *rishi* said, "*Paranci khani vyatrnat svayambhuh.*" The Lord has created man with a "manufactural defect." What is that manufactural defect? We are always seeking outside for our happiness. The *Upanishad* says that, in fact, it is not *man's* mistake; rather it is *God's* mistake that we are born like this. God could have given us "*antacaksu*" – inward vision. Instead, He has given us "*bahyacaksu.*" *Bahyacaksu* means "the sense organs." "*Tasmat paran pasyati na antaratman*" – we are not able to see our own inner Self. It is only a very few chosen people who have the clarity and heroism to gather their energies and move inward. In Vedanta, inward means upward, and outward means downward – dissipation. The upward movement is inward and integral. The downward movement is outward and dissipative. Only a very few of us try to turn inward and discover our roots so that we can experience a stable life. Now we are unstable, wandering aimlessly here and there.

An ignorant mind that at one time was seeking outside, as it becomes quiet, turns inward. Turning our minds inward is to refrain from toying with our own thoughts. It is refraining from indulging in old thoughts and going beyond the mind. Whenever we sit quietly, we generally indulge in old thoughts. This is not turning inward. You must have heard that famous story of Narcissus, who, having seen his reflection in a pool of water, was so enamoured that he sat there for the rest of his life and died. This kind of preoccupation with one's own body is known as "narcissism." We are not talking about such a preoccupation when we talk about turning inward.

Another false notion is that by turning inward one becomes an introvert, that is, one who sits down and indulges only in his private thought. Meditation is not this kind of introversion. Some people say that you have to be an introvert in order to take up meditation. We are not talking about this kind of introversion when we speak of meditation. Introversion is a disease. Narcissism is a disease. Such a mind is a diseased mind. Meditation is going beyond the mind and handling the mind with confidence and understanding. *"Kaschit dhirah pratyagatmanam aikshat / avrtta caksur amrtatvam icchan"*: "Few gather their energy, sit quietly, and turning inward discover their roots, drawing energy from their own source." When this occurs, one becomes a contented and creative person. Meditation is a way of living a free, happy and creative life.

Mind mediates between Consciousness and the world. The mind that wanders outside is the seeking mind. The mind that turns inward discovers its roots and becomes an illuminated mind. We find that mind full of light. It is that mind which is able to invoke energy from inner dimensions.

Every human being seeks two other things besides happiness – it seeks health and intelligence. Where can we get health? Generally, we think that health comes from medicine. Medicines are only placebos. Medicines cannot do anything. If it is allopathic medicine, it may even harm us. To kill one cancerous cell, a medicine may damage the whole organ. Like the Nambudri who tried to kill a rat by burning down his whole house – the rat ran away, and the house was gutted. In the same way, if we take more medicine, we become weak, our hair falls out, and the rest of our lives we must continue to live with these medicines. Though we take medicine to live, the intelligent doctor will only give placebos. A placebo means "that which builds confidence."

Some people suffering from the same disease were divided into two groups. The appropriate medicine for the disease was given to one group of people. The other set of people were given only sugar pills. Both thought that they were taking medicine. Later, *both* the groups were cured of the disease. So one group was given real medicine, and the other was given placebos, yet both groups were helped! Health is the power of the Spirit.

Intelligence is another object of human pursuit. One may read and gather a lot of information, but this reading should be done intelligently. Information should become the light of knowledge. Mere reading is just a burden. Like a bottle of kerosene oil kept in darkness, accumulation of information alone will not give us any light. The kerosene oil passing through the wick, when lit, gives us light. Mere reading is just oil without benefit of the light of knowledge. Mere accumulation doesn't serve the purpose. Mere information can only be a burden. For a donkey, a bundle of sandalwood is only a burden; but for us, sandalwood is a fragrance. For a person who has not processed information in meditation, reading does not become the All-Seeing Light. So, this light, which is intelligence, has to arise from within.

These three values that we are seeking – happiness, health and intelligence – have to manifest from within. Like the beauty of the flower latent in the seed: the seed sprouts, becomes a sapling, brings out leaves, and finally the flowers come. Where were those flowers? Those flowers were in the seed, latent in the very heart of the seed. Whatever values we fundamentally seek in life – happiness, health and intelligence – are within. Also, these values are synonymous. Health is happiness. Only a happy person can be a healthy person. Health is not merely putting on (or losing) weight. In India we have had a funny notion. We assume, "He is a very healthy person, because he is carrying excess weight," and then, one day we hear that this same person suddenly died of a heart attack! Health is happiness. Happiness is intelligence. Only a happy person can be an intelligent, all-seeing person, because he has the serenity, the tranquillity, the objectivity and the self-confidence to understand things without any ego interference.

These facts are to be understood – *that which I seek basically is within me; I have only to meditate and invoke what resides within.* That is why I have said that meditation is the highest vocation in life. Let us not simply ignore this fact. And for meditation, as we have seen, we need a non-reacting mind. With non-reaction comes meditation.

What is reaction? Reaction is the response of accumulated impressions known as memories. Memories are gathered from past experiences, be they sweet or sour. There can only be two kinds of experiences – good or bad experiences. A good experience is stored in our minds as a memory, because we want to repeat it. Isn't it? If I give you a bottle of poison and a bottle of honey, which will you choose? You will choose honey. Of course, if you contemplate suicide, then you may say that you have been searching for a bottle of poison. That is a different thing. Honey is something sweet for us. Poison is something unwanted. The past bitter and sweet experiences are stored in our minds as memory, like dust gathering on a piece of furniture. When the furniture was new, it was shiny and gleaming. After two or three days, we find there is a thick coat of dust covering it. Whenever one touches the furniture, the dust is raised, and we start sneezing. When we touch dusty and dirty furniture, all the dust and the dirt are raised. Likewise, in a mind that has gathered memories of past sweet and bitter experiences, reactions are aroused in our interactions. The mind of such a person becomes very touchy. He no longer sees the furniture, only the dust. Or our minds might be likened to a mirror full of scratches – every experience, sweet and bitter, leaves a scratch on the mirror of the mind.

Generally, what is gathered as memory is either what one is interested in or what one is mortally afraid of. If I ask you to remember a face right now, I am sure you will remember either the face of a person whom you like or one whom you dislike. We are not bothered about a person about whom we are indifferent. We are indifferent to many things because we neither like them nor dislike them. In this kind of a lifestyle, where we like and dislike, and we act accordingly, the experiences leave a mark on our minds. Unfortunately, we don't realize that. It is like plaque gathering around your teeth. But, look at a baby; his teeth are shining even though he doesn't brush his teeth. But we brush our teeth three times a day! Still we are unable to remove the plaque. Or think of a choked water pipe; there is water in the overhead tank, but it is not available in your water tap. The recollections of the past become a heavy load for you, an obstacle in your personality. It is like a blocked artery; fresh blood is unavailable to the system.

Reaction is born of the accumulated past. The past memories are of two types – psychological and technological. As humans, we operate a very complex machinery without proper instructions or knowledge of its operation. When you buy a PC and someone explains to you how you should operate it, you begin to feel sleepy. What can one do? Why bother to buy the computer, unless you want to learn how to use it properly? But we are in a different situation. You have already bought this body-mind, and it is a very complex computer. Since you are the operator, shouldn't somebody explain to you how to operate it properly? So I explain how, and again you feel sleepy. As long as you own this human computer you ought to know how to operate it.

So, memories are of two types. One is psychological memory and the other is technological memory. Technological memory includes your knowledge of mathematics, driving, cooking, etc. These are all about facts. The other kind of memory, which is psychological, is imaginary: "That person hurt me, humiliated me, insulted me; did not remember my birthday; he did not smile when he met me," etc. All these memories are gathered into our minds. When you were coming to the lecture hall, you may have seen your good friend, and he did not greet you. I am sure that throughout the class you will be thinking of him – "What kind of a person is he? He doesn't even remember all the help that I have given him. I will teach him a lesson." In the meditation class you are thinking about teaching him a lesson. This is what I call psychological memory.

In the seat of meditation, what comes as a block is not technological memory – all the mathematics, science and driving that you have learned – but the psychological memory, the insults and humiliation that have been heaped upon you. These memories are magnified and become a block for you. When we sit for meditation, we don't worry about the fact that 1+1= 2. What will we do now? Do we worry about it? No, we worry about our own personal problems.

When I say that you must rid yourselves of the past, I don't mean that you should forget your knowledge of mathematics or economics or chemistry or your telephone number. Like the person who proclaims, "Don't you know that I am a realized person?" but can't remember his own telephone number; or doesn't recall who are his children! Or one who proclaims, "I am a realized person," and then declares, "I've forgotten where my house is," and walks into another person's house that, of course, is better than his old house! If one acts like that, then one is incompetent. No intelligent man would thereafter bother to study religion. Religion should not make us less competent. Rather, true religion should make us extremely efficient and competent as persons. Moreover, when we say competent, we don't mean that you compete with somebody. One competes with himself or herself. Exploring your total potential is competition in Vedanta. When we compete with our neighbour, we may become a little wiser or wealthier than he is, but that doesn't satisfy us as spiritual persons.

So, when I say to get rid of your past, to disburden yourself of your past, what I mean is to give up, offload, the bitter psychological memories. Those memories have to be jettisoned. And the other knowledge of mathematics, physics, etc., remains part of your system. That doesn't affect one at all. Unless we forget our psychological past, our memories, no meditation is possible.

In the *Gita,* three *slokas* relevant to this situation are given:

Lokesmin dvividha nishta
pura prokta mayanagha
jnana yogena samkhyanam
karma yogena yoginam
(III.iii).

Samnyasas tu mahabaho
duhkham aptum ayogatah
yogayukto munir brahma
nacirenadhigacchati
(V.vi).

Aruruksor muner yogam
karma karanam ucyate
yogarudhasya tasyaiva
samah karanam ucyate (VI.iii)

Meditation is not easy for a disintegrated person. Meditation is not possible for a person who is always labouring under his past reactions. We must have a certain control over our reactions while we are interacting with the world. Then alone is meditation possible.

But, one might comment, "This is all theory, Sir. Can you tell me something which I should *do* from today onwards?" Having understood this idea of disburdening ourselves of the past, meditation can become a *verb* as well as a noun. As a verb, meditation refers to certain physical and psychological exercises that enhance meditation. As a noun, meditation is your very nature. To meditate, we don't have to *do* anything. We have only to relax, because the moment we *try* to meditate disturbances arise.

Now, let us deal with meditation as a verb – as something to *do*. There are five steps in meditation which one ought to practise everyday for a minimum of twenty minutes and a maximum of forty-five minutes. One should *not* practise these steps for more than forty-five minutes. Likewise, a session should *not* be less than twenty minutes. Maharshi Mahesh Yogi says that with twenty minutes of meditation each morning and evening we can solve all our problems.

And I tell you, if one per cent of an urban population meditates, they can raise the *sattva* level of that particular city. We need only that number. How many lights do you need to illumine this room? One million lights? Not necessary; one light is powerful enough. So, it follows that if we can persuade just one per cent of the city's population to meditate, we will be solving the entire city's problems. There may still be a few problematic people in the population, but they will not affect us. If meditators comprise one per cent of the population, twenty per cent of any problematic personalities can be accommodated. There will always be opposition in everything. We must have an allowance for opposition; that is all. And if one per cent of this one per cent, who are self-established, who are known as *sattvatita* (*gunatita*), then the whole country can be uplifted to empyrean heights of spiritual glory. There is no difficulty in accomplishing this. We don't have to transform the entire population. Our attempt is to transform only one per cent of the population in order to create *sattva* and 0.01 per cent to go beyond *sattva* and be established as *sattvatita*.

We have calculated that if we get three thousand people in Kerala as *sattvatita*, the entire texture of the social and creative life of this state will be transformed. At present, one per cent of the population constitutes three hundred thousand people. We must persuade three hundred thousand people to follow a *sattvic* life. And we need three thousand people who are really established in the Self. If that is achieved, the core population will become the very salt of the earth. The rest of the population will effortlessly follow them. In the ambience of an excellent person, even a stone will flower. That is the law of nature.

The Technique

We must also know meditation as a technique. As a technique it has five steps. The first step is learning to sit. Sitting is very important. Some people say that you can run and meditate, sleep and meditate, lie down and meditate, you don't have to take a bath to meditate – these are all pandering to the individual needs of the disciple and will not help. If one can lie down and meditate, why meditate at all? You can rather lie down and sleep. Can anyone meditate lying down? We may assert that we need not take a bath to meditate, since a bath creates *rajas.* But *rajas* is better than *tamas.* One should take a bath and put some *chandan* or *vibhuti* on his or her forehead. *Chandan* and *vibhuti* have great importance in activating the frontal region of the brain, the seat of intelligence. This simple technique will activate your whole system. It is for this reason that the *rishi* meditates on the *bhrumadhya*, the central region of intelligence.

When we sit in a particular posture, all the nerve centres, or the energy centres in our system, are touched and activated. (We will deal with this aspect later on). First, one has to learn how to sit cross-legged with the vertebral column erect, eyes half-closed with your hands resting on your knees. This posture, as mentioned earlier, is known as *sukhasana.* Patanjali says that "*sthirasukhamasanam*" is first step in meditation. Generally, yoga or meditation has been taken as an elaborate system of *asanas.* Most people get stuck there. To many people a *yogi* means one who can twist his body in unbelievable contortions. This type of person is supposed to be a *yogi*, but *asana* is only the *first* step in meditation. The true meditator must dispense with this step quickly and should not remain stuck there.

Step 1: First one has to sit in a particular posture – *asanam.* This, itself, will give one a lot of joy. One doesn't have to chant nor do *pranayama.* Just sit with your eyes gently closed, without any effort (the optic muscles should not be exercised), fixing your attention on the *bhrumadhya* and attending to the breath coming in and going out. This posture is known as "*sthirasukhamasanam*" (a steady, comfortable posture). Some people can sit in a *padmasana* steadily but are not comfortable. After sitting in *padmasana* for half an hour, twenty people are required to unlock his limbs and help him to stand up again! That is not the meaning of the *asana.* One must be able to manage on one's own. That is the very meaning of meditation. You must be able to get into *padmasana* and also to get out of it. Otherwise, better not to attempt this *asana.* Patanjali doesn't prescribe *padmasana* for meditation. He prescribes only *sukhasana. Sukhasana* means locking the legs with maximum spread of limbs and maximum base.

Step 2: After *asana*, the second step in meditation is *pranayama.* Essentially, we *are* the *prana.* All our physical, physiological and psychological activities are controlled by *prana*. Suppose *prana* is weak; would you be able to lift your hand? You would be unable to move at all, because *prana* is locked somewhere. That is paralysis. To unblock the *prana*, one has to breathe deeply. That is all one has to do (but not after a paralytic attack). Our whole problem is the notion that a cure comes *after* disease. Good health must derive from preventive measures not simply curative techniques.

Pranayama can open all the channels in our system. There are about 727,210,201 *nadis* in our system. One *nadi* comes from Consciousness into the *sahasrara cakra*. The *sahasrara* is constantly nourished by Consciousness. Unfortunately, we are focused somewhere in the *muladhara cakra*. Therefore, a gap occurs between the *sahasrara*, which is constantly nourished, and the *muladhara* from where we are operating. *Prana* is the controlling force. When *prana* goes, one's limbs cannot move and the metabolism cannot function. It is *prana* that governs and controls our physical system. After the departure of the *prana*, we say, "He breathed his last". Then even if we were to push a *laddu* into his mouth, it would not go down. *Prana* determines our metabolism. *Prana* determines our psychological activities, too. When *prana* goes, can we think? No, so *prana* is the guiding principle behind metabolism and all psychological and physical activities. *Prana* is the root that controls these shoots. This *prana* has five functions – to help you intake the food, digest the food, distribute the essence of food, assimilate it and excrete whatever is not necessary for the system. The physical and physiological activities are the shoots of *prana.* Breathing in and breathing out are external expressions of *prana,* and these two activities represent only the tip of the complex *pranic* system. According to the Indian *rishis, pranayama* can accomplish all that is good for the body. It can give us health, a good appetite, good digestion, good blood circulation, etc. It can free us from all diseases. All of today's civilizational, lifestyle diseases – like cancer, blood pressure, blood sugar, stomach ulcers and kidney problems – can be solved by simple, daily *pranayama.*

Step 3: The third step in meditation is the chanting of *mantras.* Words have great powers of vibration. When I produce a word, I create a vibration. It is interpreted as a positive or negative vibration. Some say that when there is a positive vibration, inevitably there must be a negative vibration. It is like saying, "Wherever there is light there is darkness." Darkness is only the absence of light. The fact is, darkness and light cannot coexist, nor are they complementary. Similarly, there are only vibrations.

Just by chanting words alone – such as, "I am infinite consciousness" – we can experience a change in our whole system. When we say "*Sivoham,*" those simple yet profound words can change our whole system. There are various incidents establishing this fact. In one such case, doctors indicated that a certain person was to die in three months of blood cancer. She thought, "I am going to die in any case. Let me stop eating." She drank only water and chanted "*Om Nama Sivaya.*" The doctors said that, nevertheless, she would die within three months. But she didn't die – even after three years! Later, this same woman became a great *mahatma.* A *mantra* has great powers.

Step 4: Visualization is the fourth step. Visualization means that the mind becomes inspired by a beautiful form. Suppose you are very moody and somebody brings a bouquet of flowers to you. What will be the change in your disposition? Suddenly, inspiration comes to you. When a little baby walks towards you and smiles, you forget everything, because that happy face has a power to uplift you.

Step 5: The final step in meditation is silence – to invoke the power of silence.

These five steps are to be practised in every evening session or, preferably twice a day. In the coming chapters we will be discussing three concepts: concentration, contemplation and meditation, initiating you into this practice. Following that, we will be discussing the *cakras*, *nadis* and *mudras*.

The evening practical meditation session, as I mentioned earlier, ought to be for forty-five minutes. In the guided meditation sessions, we use Sanskrit words with precise meanings as presented in this text. During the meditation, some may want to use a cushion and sit on the floor. One can also sit on a chair. But I would advise, if possible, to sit on the floor in *sukhasana* for meditation practice. Have this order of five steps in your mind: *asana, pranayama, mantra, visualization and silence.* These are some of the tools that will be used during our meditation. You will wonder how you spent forty-five minutes without noticing the time, and meditation will be a beautiful experience.

Meditation on Cosmic Light

Mudras are designed to activate our energy centres. We have infinite power latent in us, blocked in different centres. Generally, the *sadhaka*, by *brahmacarya* and various other internal disciplines, activates those centres of power. But here we have designed a simple technique, a sequence of *mudras*. *Mudra* means a physical posture or gesture. By assuming those physical postures one is able to activate the *cakras*. We know that physical postures are correlated to our various states of mind (*bhava*). When we are angry, we assume a certain posture, make certain gestures. All the *bhavas* of the mind are manifested as physical gestures and postures. *Bhava* is the cause, and the physical gesture is the effect. From cause to the effect – in the same way, from the effect, we can create the cause. If a positive state of mind manifests corresponding physical dispositions, conversely, one may adopt a physical posture and create the corresponding positive state of mind. From the *effect* we invoke the *cause*. Performing a specific *mudra* is one way of creating cause from a certain effect, a reversal of the usual cause-effect paradigm.

There are ten *mudra*s discussed in this text that help in meditation – *sukha*, *jnana*, *dhyana*, *yoga*, *bhakti*, *saranagati*, *prapatti*, *bodha*, *prasada* and *ananda*. Let us begin by learning the basic *mudra*s we practice during meditation. A diagram of each specific *mudra* is provided in this chapter. These *mudra*s will activate different *cakras* and bring about positive energy, devotion and divinity. Try performing these *mudras* as you read the following descriptions.

The Mudras

Sukha Mudra

In *sukha mudra* we interlock our legs to give a maximum base.

Then we are compelled to sit like a pyramid. Start by placing the heel of your left foot close to the anus and the right leg over the left leg. By sitting like this, one blocks the opening of dissipation. Now you feel stable, well organized. With the legs interlocked, providing a maximum base, keep your body erect, eyes gently closed, palms resting on the knees, and your physical attention between the eyebrows, and feel the *prana* going in and going out. While your physical attention is between the eyebrows, your mental concentration should be upon the *prana*, the in-going and out-going breath. With your eyes half-closed in *ardhanilimitam*, watch the *prana*, the in-going and out-going breath. Feel the heart beat.

Jnana Mudra

Turn your palms upward, resting the backs of your hands on your knees. The index finger should touch the tip of the thumb, and the other three fingers should be held straight. This *mudra* is an expression of surrender and wholeness. In this *mudra*, we withdraw the identification with the body-mind and surrender at the feet of the Lord. When we surrender to the Lord, we become complete. The three fingers stand for *sarira*, *mana*, and *buddhi* (or *sarira*, *antahkarana* and *jagat*). Generally we identify with the body-mind-intellect complex, and that identification makes us limited persons. The thumb stands for the *Isvara* aspect of life. The other four fingers cannot function without the

thumb. The thumb is very important; used together with the fingers, picking and plucking are possible. The whole of civilization came up after we were able to use our hands. Animals cannot create a civilization since they can only walk on their limbs. They cannot work with their hands. The accusing finger (the index finger) represents the ego. Let this finger disassociate from the body-mind complex and surrender to the Lord (the thumb), just as Hanumanji surrendered to Rama. Earlier Hanumanji was the unemployed minister of the unemployed King Sugriva, but once he surrendered to Rama, nothing was impossible for him.

Dhyana Mudra

Bring the left hand towards the navel with the right hand resting on the left hand. This is known as *dhyana mudra*, the famous posture of the Buddha. After the brain, the navel is the next major nerve centre in the body. In fact, it is also called "the second brain." When we are very angry, or when there is tremendous fear, don't we feel butterflies fluttering in the stomach?

Yoga Mudra

Raise your left hand towards the chest, near the heart. Place the right hand, with the four fingers held tightly in a fist and the thumb held erect, on top of the left hand. Let the thumb jut out, showing your will power. The nerves of these fingers are all connected to the brain. When you hold your fist tight, the brain gains a sense of discipline.

Bhatki Mudra

There is a spark of devotion and divinity in us, though we generally have not explored it. The *bhakti mudra* is designed to bring that spark of devotion alive and aflame. The *bhakti mudra* will activate your root *cakra*, the *muladhara.* Bring your hands to the level of the heart with the palms pressing together and elbows protruding to the side.

Keep your attention always on the *prana.*

Saranagati Mudra

Lift your hands up over your head, with the palms of the hands together, in a steeple form – sitting like a pyramid with the eyes gently closed. A pyramid is a powerful energy centre of the universe – like the steeple of a church or the *gopuram* of a temple. Lift your hands and tilt your chin a little upwards. You may feel a bit of strain on your muscles, but this is all right. In *saranagati mudra* you are taking refuge at the feet of the Lord of the Universe.

Prapatti Mudra

Open your hands towards heaven and, while keeping the physical eyes closed, turn your inner gaze upwards. Feel the clouds passing and the shower of blessings descending upon you. In *prapatti mudra* we offer ourselves in total surrender at the Lord's feet.

Bodha Mudra

Place the palm of your left hand at the back of your head, just above the neck. Place your right hand over the left and stretch the elbows outwards. This *mudra* is very relaxing and creates an overall feeling of well-being.

Prasada Mudra

Hold your hands open,
lightly touching the chest.
The hands touching together form
a receptacle for receiving blessings.
In *prasada mudra*
we open ourselves to receive grace from the Divine.

Ananda Mudra

Let the hands go back to the original position of *sukha mudra.* Now, without parting the lips, smile as if you are seeing the Lord. You are so joyous in seeing the Lord that you just smile. This is known as *ananda mudra.* Some may burst out into laughter – that is, if they have no control. That is why we say not to part the lips.

These technical names of *mudras* will appear once again during the instructions for the meditation. The sequence of *mudras* provided here is the prescribed order generally recommended for beginners. As you progress, this order may be modified according to the flow of the meditation.

Other Meditation Techniques

Pranayama

Pranayama is also part of our meditation sequence. First hold the left nostril with the ring finger of your right hand and breathe in through the right nostril. Then hold both nostrils momentarily and retain the breath inside for a few seconds. Release the left nostril and breathe out. Then again close both the nostrils using the same two fingers. Pause, and then open the right nostril again and breathe in. Retain the breath, as before. Then hold the right nostril and breathe out through the left nostril. Repeat this 6 to 11 times.

Inhalation is known as *purakam.* The outward breath is known as *recakam.* Retaining the air inside is known as *antakumbhakam.* Retaining the air outside is known as *bahyakumbhakam.* Notice that, unlike alternate nostril breathing, the practice I describe here is always repeated in a clockwise manner, always breathing in the same nostril and out the other.

The Chanting of Aum

Next one should chant *Aum* three to eleven times. We begin *pranayama* with *Aum* and end with *Aum. Aum* is to be chanted in a certain way – with *arohana* and *avarohana,* raising and lowering the pitch of the chant. *Aum* should not be chanted like a rocket being launched. It should be chanted from the stomach and not from the throat. When you breathe in, the stomach region below the diaphragm should extend outward; and when you breathe out, the stomach region retracts. Pause a few moments after breathing in and before chanting *Aum* with the out-going breath.

The Gayatri Mantra

We also use *mantras* as part of our meditation sequence. The *mantra* that we chant in this particular meditation is called the *Gayatri mantra.* A *mantra* is to be chanted properly. *Mantra* not only has a meaning, but *mantra* is a reservoir of energy. It is like electricity. Electricity has no inherent meaning, but when you come in contact with an electric current, you get a shock. This is the only meaning of electricity. Ordinary words have meaning; they indicate objects, but *mantra* is energy. Therefore, one must chant a *mantra* with the right accent, with the right *udata, svarita* and *anudata* (i.e. modulating the pitch in a higher, normal or lower range). Otherwise, by chanting with an incorrect emphasis, the energy will not be fully activated.

Now chant the Gayatri mantra*:*

Aum bhur bhuva svaha
tat savitur varenyam
bhargo devasya dhimahi
dhiyoyona prachodayat

Rg Veda, III.lxii.x.

Visualization

The next step in meditation is visualization. Every *mantra* has a *devata*. *Gayatri* is the *devata* of *Gayatri Chandas* (*mantra*). *Gayatri* is the Sun-God in a feminine form. In Indian culture everything is feminine except the Supreme Lord. *Gayatri* is envisaged in a feminine form. During this visualization, we are to see the Sun seated in a chariot drawn by seven horses. Otherwise, you may visualize goddess *Gayatri*, with her five heads and holding the insignias of her powers in her ten hands, seated on a red lotus.

Meditation

Preliminary Instructions

Now, let us sit for ten minutes in *sukhasana.*

After that, for another five minutes, we will chant *Aum.*

Throughout this meditation of forty-five minutes we will be sitting in *sukhasana* with our eyes closed.

For forty-five minutes you are not the body but the *prana.* All your activities are *pranic* activities. The body cannot do anything when the *prana* goes. Therefore, you are the *prani.*

Prani means *prana yasya asti iti prani* (i.e. one who breathes). Concentrate on the *prana.* Identify with the *prana.*

In closing your eyes for forty-five minutes you will develop a sense of trust. Once you have surrendered to the Lord, why be afraid of anything at all? Closing the eyes is a means of developing trust in the Universal Lord – "I am at His feet; I am taken care of. Nothing can harm me." You have only to sit.

You may be thinking, "If a mosquito comes, what will I do?" Mosquitoes will be blown away. You may be just thinking that there is a mosquito, but, in fact, there is no mosquito. But since you are restless, you may feel that there is a mosquito.

Let anything happen. For these forty-five minutes we keep our eyes closed. Whatever energy you have created will be dissipated if you open your eyes. If you unfold your legs, energy will likewise be dissipated. So fold the limbs in *asana* and close the eyes so that there is no energy dissipation or distraction at all. This is the discipline with which you are now going to sit for meditation.

We will be chanting *Aum* for five minutes, then practicing the *mudras* for another five minutes. Do the *mudras* according to my guidance.

You will be doing *mudras* while chanting the *Gayatri mantra*. Then we practice the visualization. Thereafter, we will observe five minutes of silence. In that silence you will be sitting absolutely quiet. There will be no chanting, no visualization. You will be like a drop of water falling from a leaf into the vast ocean.

Meditation Practice

Sitting in the right posture – legs interlocked, hands resting on the knees, vertebral column held erect, and with your eyes gently closed – concentrate on the *prana*, the in-going and out-going breath.

Now you are just the *prana* – not the body – when you breathe in, *you* come back along with the *prana*. Identify with the *prana* – become the *prana*.

Prana is the first manifestation of God: "*Vayo tvameva pratyaksam Brahmasi, tvameva pratyaksam Brahma vadisyami*" *(Taittiriya Upanishad, I.i.i.).*

When you concentrate upon the *prana*, you are concentrating on the first manifestation of God – the *Guruvayu,* the *Mukhyaprana.* At this stage one feels very light – you don't feel the body at all. The body is completely forgotten. You hear external sounds, but they don't disturb you.

Let the eyes remain closed. At this state you feel as light as a feather, as light as a dry leaf – you experience a kind of flowingness, weightlessness.

This *prana* is the same in all – when you breathe out, *you* go out. We breathe out what the trees breathe in. We breathe in what the trees breathe out. Experience that invisible connection between you and the tree. The tree is your life-giving God.

Chanting of *Aum*:

Having said that you are *prana* and identified with *prana*, now chant *Aum.*

Chanting is an activity of *prana. Prana* that touches various centres of the vocal chords produces the sound. When you chant *Aum*, feel that the *prana* is being activated.

Feel the *prana* becoming ablaze. All the blocks in the *nadis* will be dissolved with the chanting of *Aum.* In group sessions, I chant *Aum* first, while you listen; then you follow by chanting the *mantra*.

We will chant *Aum* five times:

Aum...Aum...Aum...Aum...Aum...

Feel the all-flowing current of *prana* – a certain light filling your inner being.

Keep your eyes closed. Don't unlock your legs or move your body; assimilate that energy.

The *Mudras*

Practice the *mudras* without chanting. There should be some pause while practicing each successive *mudra.*

Begin by letting your hands rest upon your knees in *sukha mudra.* Pause for some time in this *mudra.*

Then turn your palms upward and let the thumbs and forefingers of each hand touch in *jnana mudra,* and pause for some time.

Now slowly bring your left hand towards the navel. Then place the right hand on top of the left hand in *dhyana mudra.*

Again pause for some time. Concentrating on the *prana,* lift the left hand upwards towards the heart.

Plant the right hand atop the left hand and form a fist with the thumb protruding upwards in *yoga mudra.*

Pause once again in this posture.

Place your hands together, at the level of the heart, in *bhakti mudra.* Pause for a few moments.

Then lift your hands over your head to a steeple form in *saranagati mudra.* Feel that you have become a flame of fire leaping upwards – lifting your energy upwards. Mentally let energy – the *prana* within you – leap upwards. Again, pause in this *mudra.*

Now open your arms towards the heavens in *prapatti mudra* and pause. Relax in *bodha mudra*, with your palms placed at the back of your head. After some time drop your hands onto the knees in *jnana mudra* with the index finger touching the thumb and the other fingers held straight. All these have to be done with great care and attention – like the gentle and silent opening of a flower – move slowly and smoothly.

Hold your open palms out.

Receive the blessings of the Universal Lord – feel that you are receiving His blessings in *prasada mudra*.

Again pause for some time.

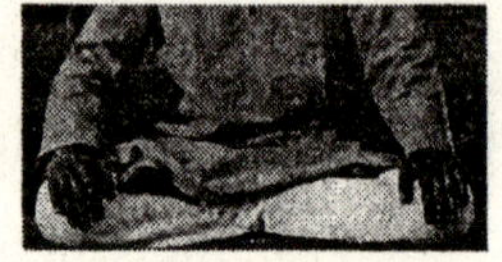

Now, slowly place your hands onto your knees and smile without parting the lips in *ananda mudra*.

Retain this *mudra* for some time.

Begin practicing *pranayama* – breathing in and breathing out six times.

Follow the flow of your breath, not your thoughts.

We have completed one round of *mudra* practice while sitting in *sukhasana*. Keeping your eyes closed, feel the inner light. Feel the vibrations throughout your body.

Mantra and *Mudra* together

Now, sitting in *sukhasana*, with your hands in *sukha mudra*, let us begin chanting the *Gayatri*. In our group sessions, I chant, and then all others follow, responding with the same chant. Please wait until I stop chanting before you begin reciting the *mantra*. When you are practicing on your own, chant the *mantra* three times, performing each *mudra* successively.

Now let us recite the *Gayatri mantra* three times while practicing each *mudra*:

Aum bhur bhuva svaha... (group chanting)
tat savitur varenyam... (group chanting)
bhargo devasya dhimahi... (group chanting)
dhiyoyona prachodayat... (group chanting)

(Repeat 3 times)

Keeping your eyes closed, turn your hands over, still resting them on the knees in *jnana mudra*. The index finger should touch the thumb:

Aum bhur bhuva svaha... (group chanting)
tat savitur varenyam... (group chanting)
bhargo devasya dhimahi... (group chanting)
dhiyoyona prachodayat... (group chanting)

(Repeat 3 times)

Now bring your hands to the navel, the right hand above the left and in *dhyana mudra*:

Aum bhur bhuva svaha... (group chanting)
tat savitur varenyam... (group chanting)
bhargo devasya dhimahi... (group chanting)
dhiyoyona prachodayat... (group chanting)

(Repeat 3 times)

Now lift your hands towards the heart in *yoga mudra*. Hold the right hand in a tight fist firmly planted on the left hand with your thumb protruding upward. Turn your chin a little upward, and hold your attention on the *prana*. With your eyes closed and your body erect, chant the *Gayatri mantra*:

Aum bhur bhuva svaha... (group chanting)
tat savitur varenyam... (group chanting)
bhargo devasya dhimahi... (group chanting)
dhiyoyona prachodayat... (group chanting)

(Repeat 3 times)

Now bring the hands together in *bhakti mudra*. Keep your eyes gently closed:

Aum bhur bhuva svaha... (group chanting)
tat savitur varenyam... (group chanting)
bhargo devasya dhimahi... (group chanting)
dhiyoyona prachodayat... (group chanting)

(Repeat 3 times)

Now open your hands and stretch out your arms towards heaven in *saranagati mudra*, as though you are supplicating before the Universal Mother – *Gayatri*, the Goddess of the

Universe, so that Her glory and compassion and love descend upon you:

Aum bhur bhuva svaha... (group chanting)
tat savitur varenyam... (group chanting)
bhargo devasya dhimahi... (group chanting)
dhiyoyona prachodayat... (group chanting)

(Repeat 3 times)

Now lift your hands up in the steeple form, in *prapatti mudra.* Straighten your body. Sit like the tongue of a flame, like a pyramid, or a like a mountain peak, shooting its way upward:

Aum bhur bhuva svaha... (group chanting)
tat savitur varenyam... (group chanting)
bhargo devasya dhimahi... (group chanting)
dhiyoyona prachodayat... (group chanting)

(Repeat 3 times)

Now rest your palms at the back of your head, right upon left, with your elbows stretched outwards, in *bodha mudra*:

Aum bhur bhuva svaha... (group chanting)
tat savitur varenyam... (group chanting)
bhargo devasya dhimahi... (group chanting)
dhiyoyona prachodayat... (group chanting)

(Repeat 3 times)

Bringing your hands to the level of the heart, open your palm towards *Gayatri Devi*, the Universal Mother, to receive her blessings in *prasada mudra*:

Aum bhur bhuva svaha... (group chanting)
tat savitur varenyam... (group chanting)
bhargo devasya dhimahi... (group chanting)
dhiyoyona prachodayat... (group chanting)

(Repeat 3 times)

Gently place your hands on the knees and smile, without parting your lips, in *ananda mudra*:

Aum bhur bhuva svaha... (group chanting)
tat savitur varenyam... (group chanting)
bhargo devasya dhimahi... (group chanting)
dhiyoyona prachodayat... (group chanting)

(Repeat 3 times)

Chant *Aum* three times, and slowly open your eyes to see a new, beautiful world!

Flowing Meditation

The word "meditation" is a much misinterpreted word. The exact Sanskrit word for meditation is *dhyana*. When this word, *dhyana*, went to China, it became *chan*. From there, it went to Japan and became *zen*. Zen has become very popular, nowadays, all over the world. *Zen* is the Japanese corruption of the Sanskrit word *dhyana*.

Another word used for meditation is *nididhyasana*. You may have come across the words "*nididhya asanam.*" *Nididhyasana* means sitting quietly. Whether it is *nididhyasana, dhyana, chan* or *zen,* they all mean the same thing. The Western vocabulary uses the words reflection, contemplation and meditation.

Reflection

Reflection means to be quiet and reflect like a mirror, without interference. Why the word *reflection*? Reflection is a quality of the mirror. If a mirror is placed in front of you, the mirror will honestly, sincerely reflect your face without interpreting it. The mirror doesn't interpret the object. The mirror only reflects the object. In other words, the mirror doesn't bring its own ideas, biases and prejudices into the presentation of the object. That is the meaning of the word *reflection*. When an ordinary person sees an object, he brings his ego, his past, his biases and his prejudices into the re-presentation of the object, that is, an interpretation rather than bias-free presentation. For example, someone might ask, "What is your idea about him?" The other replies, "He is a *raksasa*." Ask another person the same question, and he might say that this same person is an angel. To one person he is a devil; to another person he is an angel. Actually, we are seeing our own faces. When we say that he is a devil what we mean is, "I am a devil," because we bring *our* interpretation into the objects which we see.

Reflection means to be like a mirror. In the same way, a meditator should have the capacity to reflect an object *as it is*. One's consciousness should be absolutely mirror-like. A mirror-like consciousness alone has the power to reflect outside objects *as they are*. Then one establishes the right kind of relationship with the world. And, unless we establish the right kind of relationship, we will be unable to relate and to harmonize with the world. Unless we are in harmony with the world, our spiritual awakening is impossible. A person who is in constant conflict with the world cannot expect a spiritual awakening in his life because most of his energy is wasted in quarrelling over meaningless things. A capacity to eliminate unnecessary thoughts and to focus on the central object of your pursuit is necessary in meditation. A certain clarity about the world is necessary. These are the implications of the word *reflection.*

Let us consider the other terms which we come across, words like introspection, concentration, contemplation, and lastly, meditation. We ought to understand the meaning of all these words. *Intro* means "inside." *Spect* means "to watch." *Introspection* means "observing from the inside." Rather, it is observing the inside *and* observing from the inside. Who is an inspector? One who inspects or watches everything. The simple meaning of introspection is "observing from the inside."

In our tradition, Patanjali is the master of meditation. You may have heard about the *Yoga Sutras* of Patanjali like the *Brahmasutras* of Vyasa. There are about 195 *Yoga Sutras* and the first begins with "*Atha yoganusasanam.*" In the *Yoga Sutras,* Patanjali elaborately discusses the techniques, the methods and the purpose of meditation. I do not intend to discuss Patanjali's *Yoga Sutras* here but just want you to know that our tradition has a very concise and comprehensive textbook on meditation.

Patanjali begins his *Yoga Sutras* with the statement, "*Yogas citta vrtti nirodhah.*" That is Patanjali's definition of meditation.

Nirodhah means cessation, ending, coming to a state of absolute stillness. Thus, he defines meditation as "the cessation of thought modifications."

"When thoughts cease" – *citta vrtti nirodhah* – one experiences a state of mind in which there are no thought modifications. If there are thoughts, then your concentration is gone. There are no thoughts in an elevated state. Then you feel a stream of energy moving into you – you feel energized. There is no other way of energizing, except by being in a thought-free state. Patanjali says that when the mind is free from thoughts, "*Tada drastuh svarupe avasthanam,*" that mind – *svarupe avasthanam* – comes to abide in its own infinitude. No effort is required to come upon your own infinitude. You collapse into Truth naturally. You experience some mighty energy enthralling you and drawing you inwards, something like a rocket launching its inventory into the atmosphere of the moon. The rocket pushes the inventory out of the gravitational pull of the earth. For that it needs tremendous boosting power. The rocket, using its boosting power, escapes the gravitational pull of the earth and launches its inventory into vast space. In outer space there is no resistance. Only a gentle nudge is necessary, giving direction. Finally, the inventory comes into the atmosphere of the moon. What happens thereafter? The inventory is drawn towards the centre of the moon. There is no effort at all.

In meditation, also, we find these three stages. The first stage requires real effort. We have to put in a lot of effort in order to pull ourselves from the gravitational attraction of the body and the world. Once we break the gravitational pull of the body, then we experience no friction at all. There we move about for some time, until we get a nudge in some direction. That is all. Likewise, when you come into the orbit of the Supreme Self, you experience a great hand catching hold of you, drawing you into the centre of Reality. You are effortlessly drawn into the experience.

Those who meditate deeply must have experienced these three states: first, earnest individual effort; then, a frictionless plateau of calm recollectedness; and, finally, the descent of grace.

In the first state of meditation which requires great personal effort, the first obstacle we have to win over is sleep. People generally eat a lot before meditation thinking that a lot of effort is necessary – taking four omelets, two cups of milk, two bananas, an apple and two or three biscuits. I guarantee, this person will fall asleep, instantly! No one is able to meditate with such a full stomach. Instead, the stomach should be absolutely empty or, at most, one may have just a cup of hot tea.

So one has to struggle with the first obstacle in meditation, which is sleep. Next you come to a placid state or plateau where you can quietly move. And, finally, when you reach the critical mass in meditation, you experience a quantum leap, a total transformation that is not of your effort but out of some grace falling upon you and pulling you. Patanjali calls this event *dharmamegha samadhi* – a benediction, like flowers showering upon us from above bringing total transformation. This is how Patanjali describes the final fulfillment of meditation.

Friends, we have these three words – concentration, contemplation and meditation. Under the heading of contemplation we can include introspection and reflection. Reflection, introspection and contemplation essentially mean the same thing. We will come to see how these terms are synonymous.

Concentration, Contemplation, Meditation and *Samadhi*

Concentration

Let us begin with concentration. People have a notion that concentration is meditation. In fact, concentration is only the *beginning* of meditation. Concentration is not the *end* of meditation. Generally, when we say concentration, it implies what we practice in *upasana.* You take a particular *upasyadevata,* let us say Suryadevata or Ganapati or Hanuman. That particular *upasyadevata* is meditated upon by the *upasaka*. First, make an effort to concentrate upon the *upasyam* by narrowing down your area of concern and concentrating on a particular object – *cittasya desa bandhata.* The *upasaka* brings his attention from various other activities – his family, his community, his job, etc. – and gathers, or *recollects*, his mental attention. Gradually, he reduces the focus of his attention. By narrowing and gathering his energy, he finally focuses upon that particular object – be it Ganesa, Hanuman or *Devi*. One whc gathers his mental energy and focuses upon a particular object is known as an *upasaka*. The deity is called the *upasyam*. This stage is called *upasana*.

An *upasaka* is one who tries to concentrate; *upasyam* is the object on which he is concentrating; and, *upasana* is the activity of concentrating. A stage comes where *svarupa sunyam iva arthamatra nirbhasa*. *Svarupa sunyam* – the *upasaka* disappears and the *upasyam* alone remains; the meditator completely merges into the object of meditation. Ultimately, the deity alone remains. This is one way of concentration.

In concentration you are focusing upon an object other than and greater than yourself. The object of concentration should be greater than you are, otherwise, there will be no *upasana*. If you concentrate on an object lower than you, it is indulgence, not *upasana*. We constantly do such *upasana* – *laddu upasana*, cinema *upasana*. That is not *upasana*! There is no elevation. There is no enlightenment in that *upasana*. It is not that you are incapable of *upasana*. Rather, you are incapable of focusing upon higher and higher objects of concentration. True *upasana* draws upon more and more of your inner resources. All those resources which remain untapped can be drawn by you, *if* you put your goals higher and higher, *if* your object of meditation becomes higher and higher.

Concentration is, thus, focusing upon a chosen activity or object. It can be a deity, or it can be an activity. For instance, a mathematics professor needs concentration. He needs a capacity to concentrate upon the mathematical problems unaffected by his family, national or social problems. What affects our concentration is emotional turbulence. You must have experienced it. Why aren't you able to concentrate upon a chosen activity or object?

According to modern science, our brain's right and left hemispheres have different functions. The left side of the brain is the seat of reason, the seat of calculation and structuring. It is the seat of the conscious mind. The right side of the brain is the seat of passion. It is the seat of emotions and unstructured thoughts, our unconscious, our past memories, our love, our hatred – all these are embedded in the right side of the brain. Unfortunately, there is little coordination between these two sides. When passion surges in us, our reason runs away. Don't we say, "His passion took away his reason?" We have to establish a certain coordination between the two hemispheres of the brain, between passion and reason. Mere reason is insufficient. Reason may give us a direction, but, without passion, there is no movement. There are certain dry, logical people. They have no drive in life. There are passionate people, too, who have no direction in life. Both types eventually have problems.

We need passion for drive and momentum. We need reason for a direction and purpose. A person who has harmonized these two aspects of his life, reason and passion, the conscious and the unconscious, can alone lead a successful and reasonably fulfilling life. We cannot divorce these two aspects of personality. Modern science has discovered that if, by *upasana*, we create a network between these two aspects of the brain, then certain new channels are created. Then one is passionate, with plenty of energy, and reasonable also.

The problem with the modern human being is that he is merely reasonable with no control over his passions. He is an expert doctor, an expert engineer, an expert computer scientist or an expert mathematician. He has no control over his passions. For example, a man is about to go to his office. The roads are smooth and clear. His office is only two miles away. But before that, when he was about to take leave of his wife, she did not look at him but instead turned her face the other way. She asked him for something, but, in his hurry, he forgot about it. Finally, they argued over this when he was ready to go to the office. She issued an ultimatum: "Either me or your office." His mind became turbulent and reason abandoned him. He was unable to make up his mind. At that time, when he drives to work, what will be his condition? I am sure he will have a few problems on his way to the office. Maybe even a mishap; may be he will hit a dog. All the time he will be disturbed because his passion is not kept under control. If our passion is not kept under control, none of our rational expertise will be of help.

There should be a harmony between passion and reason. Don't think that Vedantins are people without passion. They are highly passionate people, but their passion has a direction and purpose. Their passion is like a flame moving upwards. Their passion is not like water flowing everywhere and dissipating.

It should be understood that we need both developed and disciplined passion under the control of reason. *Upasana* means just that – bringing your energies *and* your passions to focus upon a particular object. It is the capacity to put your heart and soul into the moment's activity. It is putting your mind behind your limbs. This is concentration. When we drive, we need supreme concentration as we must attend to a lot of things. We have to apply pressure either upon the brake or upon the accelerator. Our hands are on the wheel, but we have to look in front. We have to look in the rear-view mirror also. So, we need all our senses fully alert when we drive. That is an act of concentration. When you drive you are in supreme concentration because, then, your attention never wavers.

Concentration is necessary in our daily activities, as well. Suppose you are about to go to bed. Having taken hot milk, switched on the AC, slipped into your nightwear and said your prayers, just as you were about to jump into bed, you suddenly see a black cobra in the room. You had already locked the room, but, because the snake is between you and the door, you dare not open the door either. Then what will be your state of mind the whole night? All the time you will be looking at the cobra. There you experience supreme concentration!

So concentration means focusing your attention upon a particular, chosen, limited thing. It is an activity of exclusion. You exclude everything and focus upon a chosen thing. This is the concentration that is necessary in our daily living. Modern man lacks concentration. He cannot put his heart and soul into a single stream of activity. Now, when you are listening to the speaker, you are not fully participating. Your whole being is not listening. Only a part of your mind is listening. A part of your mind is at your home or somewhere else.

The capacity to put your self totally into a chosen single stream of activity, idea or an object is concentration. Someone asked a Buddhist monk, "What is your spiritual activity? What do you concentrate upon?" He said, "My spiritual life is very simple. I have a bath early in the morning. I eat my breakfast. Then I play a little. I take a short walk. I sleep a little, and then again I play, drink and eat. Then I have my dinner and go to sleep." The man continued his inquiry, "Is this spiritual activity? If that is so, I also do it," "No," said the monk, "You are not doing it. When you play, you study. When you study, you play. When you eat, you take a bath. When you take a bath, you eat. What concentration is in that? You have no concentration at all. When you are eating, you are thinking of the office. When you are at the office, you are thinking of home." Similarly, there was someone whom everybody at home called a *sanyasi* because at home he was always talking about the *ashram*. But, at the *ashram* he was only thinking of home. Such a person lacks concentration, the coordination of his mental and physical activities.

Concentration is putting your heart and soul completely into a piece of work. When you are driving, you are concentrating on that alone. At that time you need not chant a *mantra*. If you can put yourself totally behind driving, you have attained concentration. *Mantra*, in this situation, blocks your concentration. The true *mantra* is this act of being *in* the activity. You are totally *in* the activity. A stage comes when only the driving remains and the driver disappears – *svarupa sunyam iva arthamatra nirbhasa* – you are not there, the car is not there, the roads are not there; what remains is a mingling of all these into a flame of experiencing driving. Then you have attained a kind of temporary *samadhi*. The total absorption into the particular chosen activity – this is what is meant by concentration. Concentration can be achieved in all fields of activity, be it driving, cooking, sweeping the floor, talking to somebody or whatever it might be that you are doing.

But this is not sufficient, because this mode of concentration cannot be continuous. Can you continuously drive? It's not possible. Can you continuously look at a chosen deity? Impossible! Can you continuously look at a flame? Impossible! The activity of concentration cannot be continuous, because of certain limitations of the object, the subject and the activity.

Concentration is the *first* step in meditation. Doing your work with total concentration is the *first* step in meditation. A person who cannot concentrate on his work can forget about meditation. That is why, when a person comes to me for meditation, the questions I ask are: "How is your business? How are you in your office?" And if he says, "I have no interest in the office; I only want to think of God and nothing else," that means he is an escapist. He is not a true meditator. He is hiding behind the name of meditation.

First, he has to put himself into his work. Let him make a success there. Let him learn concentration there. Be a good chef, if you are a chef. Be a good driver, if you are a driver. Whatever work we do, be it menial or the highest order of vocation, we must first be able to concentrate. So the first qualification for meditation is the capacity of concentration.

Contemplation

The next step is contemplation. It can also be called introspection and/or reflection. What are the factors that come into play, for example, in the act of seeing? There is an object upon which you are concentrating. The sense organs come into play with the mind activating them. When the mind and the sense organs are totally absorbed into an object, it is concentration. But behind the object are the sense organs. Behind the sense organs is the mind. Behind the mind there is something else continuously reflecting and illuminating all these activities.

That is the *saksi*, the witness of all these activities.

Contemplation means detached concentration, to remain cut off from the object and the mind interacting with the object. In the word contemplation, "tem" means "to cut off." A temple is a place where we cut ourselves off from the world. When you step into the temple, leaving your shoes outside, you keep the world outside also. You don't take your shoes along with you into the *sanctum sanctorum*. In the temple we can remain cut off from the world because we are in communion with the Lord. Contemplation means to remain detached from the object *and* the mind that is interacting with the object. To remain in an attitude of the witness – *saksibhava* – is contemplation. In this state, you neither completely forget yourself nor completely disappear into the act of concentration. You always know you have a greater depth, so that when the object goes and when the mind changes, you don't feel any change inside. You remain the same, deep person.

What is the process of a mental disturbance? One finds that the objects are changing. When we concentrate on a particular object, the mind is focused upon it, and the object, by its very nature, has to change. I hope you understand this point; the object, by nature, should change. When the object changes, the mind also reflects that change. As you identify with the mind – and the mind with the changing object – you feel disturbed. If you can, understand that the object will change, the mind's modifications change; but Consciousness

– that *I* which illumines the object and their interactions – does not change. Do *I* change? For example, think of a lamp: when we were not in its presence, its light illuminated the emptiness, and, when we came into the room, the light also illumined our presence. After some time, when we leave the room, the light will continue to illumine in our absence also. Despite the initial emptiness, then the presence of the people, and then again the absence of the people – the light illuminates everything without any attachment. It is not that when we arrive, the light suddenly comes into manifestation and, then, when we go the light thinks, "For whom should I shine now? Nobody appreciates me." It doesn't happen like that. This type of thought and action is only for people who strive to be noticed. If such a person wants to give a contribution to a poor man, he will see that the media are there to record the event. If they are late, he will wait for them to arrive. But the light doesn't do that. The light, whether we are there or not, illumines our presence or absence.

In the same way, there is a light of Consciousness that illuminates the presence and the absence of objects. Identifying with that source of illumination – when you look at the world, the mind and its activities – is known as contemplation. This quality of contemplation is to be cultivated. In the modern world we lack this quality of contemplation. We don't stand apart from our activities. Standing apart does not mean that we don't *do* any activity. This is another mistaken notion – "I am standing apart. That is what my *guru* has taught me. Therefore, I am not interested in anything." If you lack interest, it does not mean that you are standing apart; it is likely that you are still very much engaged mentally. Your behavior is still a *reaction*. Either you are fully involved in the world physically, or you are fully involved in it mentally. But concentration gives one depth, like the depth of the ocean; then you are not affected by anything. When you stand apart in terms of understanding, and yet continue to do everything, that is known as detached activity. Detached concentration is contemplation.

Concentration with a certain depth is contemplation. You continue driving, but at the same time you are so alert that there is a depth that goes beyond the object and the mind that is involved in the activity of concentration. Then you can say that you are contemplating.

The contemplative quality (that is the necessary quality of reflection) is the quality of introspection – the watching from the inside – necessary for meditation. Generally, when people introspect, they judge and criticize. Introspection has degenerated to that level. Introspection becomes self-flagellation. The Christian interpretation of introspection sometimes results in personal witch-hunting, "I did this wrong; I did this right," and one develops guilt feelings. Real introspection is not witch-hunting, trying to find fault with anybody – including one's own self. Real introspection is just allowing thoughts and events to take place. Thoughts flower and fade away, like clouds that come, clamour, clash and disappear. In the same way, we are to allow things to happen without any interference, without any judgment. Non-judgmental witnessing of worldly events and thoughts is contemplation, reflection or introspection. This quality of non-judgmental contemplation or witnessing is to be cultivated.

From concentration we evolve into contemplation. Practice *that* whenever you do an activity. See whether you are concentrating totally. And if you are totally concentrating, then you can also contemplate. If you are not concentrating, then you cannot contemplate because you have already made a division inside yourself. A part of your mind is somewhere else. One should develop a capacity to mingle and then gather, so that when you act, you are fresh and absolutely pure. There is then neither a feeling of effort, nor tiredness nor fatigue!

There are two types of activities. One is the activity that wears you out, which makes you tired. It is then that we keep on saying, "I have done it." We keep on reminding the other person that we have done a lot of things. Why? Because we never enjoyed what we were doing! But, if we have joy in what we are doing, we will never remember the past. It is only a person who did not truly enjoy what he did who will keep on reminding us of all the glorious things he has done. Does telling about the past give the true joy of living? Will he not constantly live in the past? We recite our old glories all the time. Why is it so? If any person recites his old glories, we can immediately understand that he did not enjoy what he did. If he really enjoyed it, he will never talk about what he did in the past, because his desire is to go into the future. Where is the time to discuss and think about the past glories? We move constantly. Constant movement is *sanyasa. Sanyasa* means to create and to leave the fruits of our work behind for lesser mortals to quarrell over and fight about. The *sanyasi* moves ahead. A *sanyasi* has no time to look back into the past; life is a constant flowering experience for the *sanyasi*. That is contemplation – creating and leaving it all behind. Detached activity is continuously flowing.

Meditation

It is in the state of detached concentration that we experience true meditation. True meditation is not concentrating upon an object outside. It is striking roots deep into your own *Self.* Take the example of a tree: when a tree grows upward with its branches and shoots, leaves, flowers and fruits, correspondingly it grows deeper. Its roots strike deeper, spreading all over. There are certain trees whose root systems spread over an area of 500 square kilometres. A tree that wants to touch the sky must have its roots deep into the very existence. If, like a bonsai tree, the roots are continuously cut back – how will it grow? It will grow only to that extent that it can be placed in a drawing room. It will have only small branches and a few leaves.

When you grow in activity from concentration to contemplation, you naturally and simultaneously experience an inward growth. That inward growth is natural – not created. That is when you will experience an inward pull. A mighty hand gathers and envelops you, hastening you into the inner recesses of existence. And that experience of total collapse into the Self, which comes naturally, is meditation. It is a deepening of your roots so that your shoots can grow. A person who is truly meditative, will be an absolutely active person in this world. We cannot say that a mighty tree has only deep roots but has no shoots. It is not possible. A true meditator is a supremely active person in this world; he is not an idle person. Our general concept of a meditator is, "Oh, he meditates a lot; he doesn't do anything else." In fact, he is not meditating but is simply sleeping. *Bhagavan* calls it *tamasic* meditation – that is, *jada dhyana* – you are like a *jada*, a piece of stone, lying down. It means that the stone also meditates as it is not talking to anyone. Simply not talking to anyone is *not* meditation; remaining inactive is not meditation, either. Meditation is *through* activity. You are fully active, but in the process you are deepening your roots, filling your entire existence. That experience is meditation.

There is concentration, contemplation, and finally, meditation. By developing the attitude of the silent witness – a non-judgmental watching of all the mind's activities in the world, not identifying with any of them – you come to a state of the true experience of meditation. Once you strike roots deep into the core of existence, then you can draw infinitely from that core. A meditator is one who has infinite energy, one who is ever energetic, ever enthusiastic, but at the same time very quiet. No unwanted word or gesture will escape from such a being. When such a person utters a word, it will have the power of the entire cosmos behind it. That is the power of a meditator. A gesture or a glance is sufficient – a thousand suns shine in one single glance. The whole universe will come to a standstill. Some of our *rishis* could stop the sun with only a gesture.

This kind of a power, energy, enthusiasm, and compassion become the natural qualities of a meditator. The meditator embodies the ultimate power of existence. A sick man comes to Him. He only has to raise His hand – the sick man will be absolutely cleansed and will bloom like a fresh flower. A leprous person with oozing wounds comes to Him; he will become as clean and pure as a little child. If He moves into a place that has had no rain for twelve years, rains will come, the ponds will be full of water, lotuses will bloom, and the spring will come along with Him. Barren women will beget children, and barren cows will give milk. The clouds will bring rain. The whole of existence will be fulfilled in His presence. With a few people like that, the whole world is transformed. These blessings are the final fruit of meditation – of concentration, contemplation and meditation.

Ashtanga Yoga

Patanjali says that there are certain steps in meditation. First come *yama* and *niyama*, certain ethical and mental dispositions. Then come *asana, pranayama, pratyahara*, and finally, *dharana, dhyana* and, *samadhi*. Together these are known as *Ashtanga Yoga*. In *yama* comes *ahimsa, satyam, brahmacaryam, asteyam* and *aparigraham*, which are the ethical values. In *niyama* comes *saucam, tapa, santosam, arjavam* and *isvarapranidhanam*. (I am just mentioning the words Patanjali uses and explains in his text.) *Asana* is *sthirasukhamasanam* – a capacity to sit quietly for forty-five minutes. Please understand that this means without a newspaper, without the TV, without chewing gum and without a telephone. Some people, having nothing else to do, make telephone calls just to ask, "How are you?" without any sense of purpose.

Can't we be alone with ourselves? Are we so afraid of ourselves? We always want to escape from ourselves. We don't want to come to terms with our own Self! Unless we come to terms with ourselves, how can we meditate? Coming to terms with one's own self means objectively knowing your own strengths and weaknesses. Everybody will have some weaknesses. The creation itself has a defect. If that condition were not there, the Lord would be unable to dissolve this creation. Consider a building, for example. Anything created lives for a limited period of time. It cannot be eternal. Even a building has a life span, as human being has a life span. God has this provision in this creation so that it can manifest. Everyone will have a few defects – *sarvarambha hi dosena dhumenagnir ivavrta*: "As fire is always enveloped by smoke, activity is enveloped by a shadow." So we have to recognize our strengths and weaknesses. This capacity to objectify is contemplation.

Coming under *niyama*, *santosa* is another great quality that Patanjali talks about – to be happy all the time. Try to smile. Someone may be your number one enemy, but give him a flower. Thereafter, his poison will become nectar. You have not lost anything by just giving a flower. The whole poison that was flooding into the world becomes nectarine fragrance. The whole thing can be transformed with a simple gesture, but our ego doesn't allow that. We know that we should do it, but we don't do it. Deliberately cultivate *santosa*.

Another great quality is austerity. It means to live a simple life. We need very few things. A simple person will live healthily and long. If we have simple habits, eat simple food and lead a simple life, we can live a healthier, longer and more creative life. That is why, according to Hindu tradition, as we go up in the hierarchy, the managing directors – the top-level people in Indian society – live a simple life. Prime Minister Lal Bahadur Shastri used to drink a glass of carrot juice for breakfast. Then at three o'clock for lunch he would eat a *chapati* and a little *dal*. At night he drank a cup of milk. And, for two years during times of great difficulty he led this country.

If we have the minimum of requirements, we can do the maximum. If we eat all the time, our whole energy is wasted in digesting what we have eaten. We store the excess as fat in our system. And, without converting our food into energy, we become a huge bag of vegetables and wheat and rice – an ugly spectacle. Why carry that load? It is not necessary. Load shedding is necessary. Shed the load. Don't we say, "Travel light and make your journey a pleasure!" We are travelling continuously with heavy burdens. Our bone structure collapses under the unnecessary weight of this garbage. We get backaches and suffer from a slipped disc. So, if we change a little, this wonderful life can be lived gloriously.

Ashtanga Yoga includes *dharana* (concentration) and *dhyana* (continuous concentration) and *samadhi*. *Dhyana* is *sajatiya vrtti pravaham dhyanam. Vrttisajatyam dhyanam* – the "flow of similar thoughts." One may continue to concentrate as long as necessary, developing the capacity to apply the mind and withdraw the mind also. Some people can concentrate, but they cannot withdraw. Unless we have supreme alertness, we cannot become creative. If we are all the time doing some petty little things, then we become petty. We don't want to become like that. We want to become people with deep multi-faceted interests, so that these interests become mutually reinforcing.

Samadhi

Samadhi is the capacity to concentrate and draw nourishment from your inner depths. This means growing roots and simultaneously growing a trunk. That is the true meaning of *samadhi*. When this state is attained you are in pure *samadhi*. Patanjali has divided *samadhi* into nine steps – *savitarka, nirvitarka, savicara, nirvicara, samprajnata, asamprajnata, sabija, nirbija* and *sahaja*. These are various states in *samadhi*, which itself can be sub-divided into *bahya, antara, bahya sabdanuviddha, antara sabdanuviddha, bahya drsyanuviddha and antara drsyanuviddha*. I use all these words not to impress you, but just to tell you that we have done a lot of research into this matter. So much research has been done into the very nature of *samadhi* itself that even a slight wrong note can be understood. Like an Eskimo who can identify different types of snow, having lived in such an environment, or an American who can identify over two hundred types of ice cream, *samadhi* is fine-tuned to ultimate perfection.

In *samadhi* itself there are various states. A state comes when *samadhi* is your natural state – *nirbijasahaja samadhi*. *Nirbija* means that one who attains this type of *samadhi*, who thereafter never comes out of this state – he perpetually enjoys that state. There is no distraction whatsoever. These are some of the things we need to understand in terms of meditation. In the following chapters I will be discussing *kundalini*, the *cakras*, the Universal Mother, and communicating with the Compassionate Lord through meditation.

Meditation on Cosmic Consciousness

Meditation Practice: Now let us begin the meditation. During this meditation we have to sit in *sukhasana* and keep our eyes closed for forty-five minutes. This is the only way to develop trust in the Lord. When we open our eyes and look around, first, we become distracted and, secondly, there is distrust. When we close our eyes, the ego melts and we experience trust. So, we start by closing our eyes.

Interlock your legs and rest your hands on the knees.

Holding your body erect, draw your mental attention to the point between the eyebrows – the *brhumadhya*. And, through the *brhumadhya*, focus your attention continuously on the in-going and out-going breath.

You are not this body. You are the *prana*.

Feel that you are the *prana*. Once the *prana* goes, the body is dead, and a dead body is of no use. What makes the difference is the *prana*. Therefore, *you* are the *prana*. This *prana* is the governing energy of the body-mind complex. The physical, physiological and psychological activities are all controlled and governed by this *prana*.

It is the *prana* that helps us receive information through the five sense organs.

When we eat, swallowing is possible because of the *prana*. When we see, vision is possible because of the *prana*. All the information impinging upon us through the five sense organs is possible because of the *prana*. It is this *prana* that helps us digest what we have eaten. It is this *prana* that helps us circulate what we have digested. It is this *prana* that helps us assimilate what is circulated. It is this *prana* that helps us excrete.

This *prana* is God's manifestation in our life going through all the 727 million *nadis*.

Inhalation and exhalation are the outward expressions of the *prana*, but this is only the tip of an iceberg. It is that deeply-rooted *prana* with which you are to identify.

The *Taittiriya Upanishad* says in brief, "O *Prana*, I see you as the manifested form of the Lord."

Namaste vayo
tvameva pratyaksam brahmasi
tvameva pratyaksam brahma vadisyami
rtam vadisyami
satyam vadisyami
tanmamavatu tadvaktaramavatu
(*Taittiriya Upanishad*, Invocation)

Identify with that *prana*. When the *prana* flows out, it enters into *samasti prana*. Again, we breathe in from the *samasti prana*. To facilitate the identification with the *prana*, breathe slowly, deeply and deliberately. Retain that breath for some time. Then breathe out slowly, consciously and deliberately. Fill your lungs with air. Retain the breath inwardly for some time. Then breathe out through both nostrils. As you identify with the *prana*, your whole inside is illuminated. You feel the body is like smoke around fire. Enjoy the experience of going out of the body when you breathe out and coming into the body when you breathe in. Play with the *prana*. This *prana* is a vibration. *Prana* is light. *Prana* is life. *Prana* has no dimension or weight. It is weightless. You feel weightless and undisturbed. Outside disturbances do not bother you. Even these spoken words do not disturb you. Feel the light inside. Feel the vibration. Feel the *prana* going through all the *nadis*. This is the presence of the Universal Mother, Her touch. She lives in you and with you as the light of *prana*.

Now when we chant *Aum*, understand that chanting is an activity of the *prana*. The sound should be produced from the depth of the stomach affecting the region where the *kundalini* is lying in deep sleep. Extract *Aum* from the very depth of your stomach. As you roll out *Aum* from this depth, you find the *prana* becoming ablaze. Chant *Aum* from the very core of your being, from the pit of the stomach.

Please listen while I chant *Aum*. Then repeat the chant. Feel the vibration of the *prana*. Your whole system will vibrate as *Aum*. Every cell will throb in terms of *Aum*:

Aum... (group chanting)
Aum... (group chanting)
Aum... (group chanting)

After every chanting of *Aum* allow a moment of silence – and that silence is to be relished. Chant *Aum* and, when the silence follows, become one with that silence. Vibrate as *Aum*. It is not chanting *Aum*; it is *vibrating* as *Aum*. So *Aum* – silence – *Aum* – silence. That silence is to be appreciated and enjoyed as much as possible:

Aum... (group chanting & silence)
Aum... (group chanting & silence)
Aum... (group chanting & silence)

Now take a deep breath through both nostrils and retain it for some time. Then chant *Aum* through the mouth. Take in air through the nostrils. Do *stambhana* for a few seconds, and then breathe out through the mouth. Breathing out through the mouth again chant *Aum*. Then breathe in again through both nostrils. Retain that breath:

Aum... (breathe in – retain –)
Aum... (breathe in – retain –)
Aum... (breathe in – retain –)
Aum... (breathe in – retain –)
Aum... (breathe in – retain –)
Aum... (breathe in – retain –)
Aum... (breathe in – retain –)

When you perform the *mudras*, don't feel that they are a disturbance. Rather, *mudras* are expressions of the *prana*. When you perform a *mudra*, don't think that you are distracted. It is only the movement of *prana*. Without the *prana*, you cannot stretch your limbs. So, identify with the *prana*. Feel the *prana* activated when you stretch your limbs.

Bring your hands together in *bhakti mudra*. Keeping your eyes closed, fix your attention between the eyebrows and on the *prana*. You are *not* the body. When you bring your hands together, it is the *prana* that acts. Now chant *Aum* while doing *bhakti mudra*:

Aum... (group chanting)
Aum... (group chanting)
Aum... (group chanting)

Now, slowly and gracefully lift your hands. Stretch your

hands above your head into the steeple form, in *saranagati mudra*. Become a flame. Your energies are surging upwards. Lift your chin upwards a little. Listen and chant alternately, as before:

Aum... (group chanting)
Aum... (group chanting)
Aum... (group chanting)

Gently drop the hands onto the knees in the *jnana mudra*, still keeping your eyes closed.

Aum... (group chanting)
Aum... (group chanting)
Aum... (group chanting)

Bring your left hand slowly to the navel region in *dhyana mudra*. Resting the right hand upon the left hand, press the navel a little:

Aum... (group chanting)
Aum... (group chanting)
Aum... (group chanting)

Now you are breathing very deeply. Jump into that *prana*. Be that *prana*. Raise your hands up to the chest and heart region in *yoga mudra*:

Aum... (group chanting)
Aum... (group chanting)
Aum... (group chanting)

Open your hands into *prasada mudra*:

Aum... (group chanting)
Aum... (group chanting)
Aum... (group chanting)

Again, bring your hands together in *bhakti mudra*:

Aum... (group chanting)
Aum... (group chanting)
Aum... (group chanting)

Now gracefully place your hands upon the knees in *ananda mudra*. You smile without parting the lips. You feel a certain overflowing of light within, a certain inner "coolness" – *antasitalata* – inner coolness, inner leisure. All your muscles are totally relaxed. All your *nadis* are overflowing.

Now without opening your eyes, do some simple stretching exercises. Stretch wherever you feel tension – the limbs, the neck. You are resting on the bosom of the Universal Mother. Stretch – letting that energy flow on. May you become like the flowing energy of a flower in the breeze or the gentle swaying of a flame.

Come back to your original position, into *sukha mudra*, with your hands resting upon your knees. Relax. Observe the *prana,* the in-going and out-going breath.

Now do *pranayama* as before, in a clockwise manner: blocking the left nostril, breathe in through the right nostril. Retain the breath by blocking both the nostrils. Then release the air through the left nostril. Again, without opening the eyes, block the left nostril, taking air inside using the right nostril. Then block both nostrils and again hold the breath. Open the left nostril and breathe out. Complete six *pranayamas* in this same way.

Drop the *pranayama* practice now, and simply focus your attention between the eyebrows. Inside you feel full of light. You feel like opening your eyes and seeing the light outside. The light is inside, and you feel your whole being fully illumined. Abide in that attitude for sometime. Relax.

Now let us chant *Aum Nama Sivaya*.

As before, first listen and then chant:

Aum... Nama... Sivaya... (group chanting)
Aum... Nama... Sivaya... (group chanting)
Aum... Nama... Sivaya... (group chanting)

Bring your hands together in *bhakti mudra*. With your eyes closed, listen first and then chant:

Aum... Nama... Sivaya... (group chanting)
Aum... Nama... Sivaya... (group chanting)
Aum... Nama... Sivaya... (group chanting)

Let your eyes remain closed.

When chanting with a group, wait quietly until everyone stops chanting *Aum*. Some may take more time. Wait patiently for everyone to finish.

Now lift your hands above the head. Listen and then chant:

> *Aum... Nama... Sivaya...* (group chanting)
> *Aum... Nama... Sivaya...* (group chanting)
> *Aum... Nama... Sivaya...* (group chanting)

Open your arms towards heaven. Tilt your chin upwards. Your eyes, though still closed, are rolled upwards. Listen and then chant:

> *Aum... Nama... Sivaya...* (group chanting)
> *Aum... Nama... Sivaya...* (group chanting)
> *Aum... Nama... Sivaya...* (group chanting)

Bring your hands down upon your knees, slowly. Relax in *jnana mudra*. Listen and then chant:

> *Aum... Nama... Sivaya...* (group chanting)
> *Aum... Nama... Sivaya...* (group chanting)
> *Aum... Nama... Sivaya...* (group chanting)

Bring your hands towards the navel in *dhyana mudra*. Listen and then chant:

> *Aum... Nama... Sivaya...* (group chanting)
> *Aum... Nama... Sivaya...* (group chanting)
> *Aum... Nama... Sivaya...* (group chanting)

Bring your hands together to *bhakti mudra*.

Feel the energy, the light inside you. You feel cool. The *prana* energy is cooling. You feel ecstatic. You may even have goose bumps.

Listen and then chant:

Aum... Nama... Sivaya... (group chanting)
Aum... Nama... Sivaya... (group chanting)
Aum... Nama... Sivaya... (group chanting)
Aum... Nama... Sivaya... (group chanting)
Aum... Nama... Sivaya... (group chanting)
Aum... Nama... Sivaya... (group chanting)
Aum... Nama... Sivaya... (group chanting)

Drop your hands onto your knees and smile without parting the lips, without exercising the facial muscles. Feel the embrace of *Siva*. Feel you are hand in hand with *Siva*. Feel the laughter of *Siva* tingling all over you. Feel the embracing warmth of *Siva*.

You have left the world of worries behind. You have left the hills and valleys and reached the Himalayas. You have reached Mount Kailash. Take a cool shower in Lake Manasarovar where lotuses are in full bloom and crystals of ice reflect on the blue waters of the lake. You have left your past. You have left your worries. You have left your body. You have left your memories behind. You have crossed a range of mountain peaks and have reached the abode of *Siva*, Mount Kailash. Travel around the Mount three times. Look at the peak and see Lord *Siva* in deep meditation, smiling. See his matted hair adorned with a crescent moon. Lord *Siva* is in deep meditation. Wearing a tiger skin, his body is smeared with ashes and snakes are draped around his neck. His third eye is gently closed.

May you be transfixed in the presence of the Lord. May you lay your head there at the feet of the Lord.

You find the mountain opens. You are drawn into the womb of the mountain. You are one with *Siva*.

Now listen, and then chant *Sivoham*:

Sivoham... (group chanting)
Sivoham... (group chanting)
Sivoham... (group chanting)
Sivoham... (group chanting)
Sivoham... (group chanting)
Sivoham... (group chanting)
Sivoham... (group chanting)

As you are drawn into the depth of *Siva*, the Cosmic sound and the *mantra* recedes and ceases. You become more and more subtle. And, finally, the *mantra*, the *devata* and the mind all coalesce into one flame of blissful experience in the embrace of *Lord Siva*. You are in the Abode of *Siva*:

Aum... (group chanting)
Aum... (group chanting)
Aum... (group chanting)

Purnamada purnamidam
purnat purnamudacyate
purnasya purnamadaya
purnamevavasisyate
Aum Santih Santih Santih

(*Brhadaranyaka* & *Isa Upanishad*, Invocation)

Aum sarve bhavantu sukhinah
sarve santu niramayah
sarve bhadrani pashyantu
ma kaschit duhkhabhag bhavet
Aum Santih Santih Santih

(Ancient Sanskrit Prayer)

Aum asato ma sadgamaya
tamaso ma jyotirgamaya
mrtyorma amrtam gamaya
Aum Santih Santih Santih

(Brhadaranyaka Upanishad, I.iii.xxviii)

Now slowly open your eyes.

Kundalini Meditation

According to the Vedic vision of existence, what is primary is Consciousness or *Brahman*. *Sadeva idam agre asid*: "In the beginning there was only *Sat*," which we call Truth, Existence, God or *Brahman*. From that *Sat* – pure existence – first manifested the *trigunas (Chandogya Upanishad VI.ii.i)*. From the *trigunas* came the *pancabhutas*, and from the *pancabhutas*, by their endless permutations and combinations, arose this variegated world.

How did the *Sat*, the Truth that is beyond time, space and division, become this world of multiplicity? The "becoming" is a mystery. The *Veda* calls it *maya* – *mayaya pururupamiyade* –

"through *maya* Truth has become many." Why do we call this becoming of One into many *maya*? Because Truth, God, Consciousness, *Sat*, without undergoing any intrinsic change, has become this manifold world. This capacity of God to manifest as the entire world without undergoing any intrinsic change is known as *maya-sakti*. So *Bhagavan* is *Saktiman* – *Sakti yasya ast iti saktiman*. He has this particular power of *maya*. This is the Vedic view of creation and existence.

Regarding the first cause, in the *Rg Veda* there seems to be no definite conclusion. We don't know what was at first. "*Nasadasid nosadasid tadanim*," says one of the profound Vedic *mantras*: "Then there was neither aught nor naught." Neither *Sat* nor *asat* existed at that time. What there was at that time nobody knows. The phrase used is: Darkness coiled in darkness. There was *no* time. Towards the end the *rishis* stall the question: "What was there in the beginning?" The answer is a somewhat exasperated, "Who knows? Not even the gods know." Nevertheless, it is from there that the whole universe manifests.

There is a beautiful passage in the *Taittiriya Upanishad* (II.i) that is very revealing. The *rishi* says:

Om Brahmavidapnoti param
tadeshabhyuktah
satyam jnanamanantam brahma
yo veda nihitam guhayam parame vyoman
sosnute sarvan kaman saha
Brahmana vipasciteti

tasmadva etasmadatmana akasah sambhutah
akasadvayuh vayoragnih
agnerapah adbhya prthvi
prthviya osadhayah osadibhyonnam
annatpurusah

Here the *rishi* traces the origin of the human being. He says that the human being is born of food – *annat purusha.* If any of you doubt that, don't eat food for fifteen days; then you will also be convinced. The mind, intellect, body, memory, your ego – everything is born of food. If there is no food, there is no body experience. Therefore, *annat purusha*: "Man is nothing but food." The food that his parents ate became the ovum and the sperm which together created the first cell. The accumulated food becomes the child. The child comes out, and he again eats food and grows. So body-mind is the modification of food. Where does food come from? *Osadibhyonnam*; food comes from plants. Where do plants come from? *Prthviya osadhayah*; plants come from the earth. The sunlight and moonlight falling upon the earth makes the topsoil alluvial and fertile. Only the topsoil, seven to ten inches deep, is fertile. From where does the nourishment of the soil come? *Adbhya prthvi* – from the water. Therefore, man is nothing but food. Food is nothing but plants. Plants are nothing but earth. Earth is solely the modification of water molecules.

You are nothing but a modification of water. Seventy-five

per cent of your body is water. If you were to be completely dehydrated, what would remain is just enough powder to put in a matchbox. Someone calculated the value of the minerals and elements with which God created human beings. At present, these materials would cost only seventy-five rupees. With just a few dollars, God has created such magnificent machinery. Although we spend thousands and thousands, we are unable to create such a beautiful system. That is human folly. Whereas God spent nothing, He has created everything. That is why He is a *Yogi*. We spend everything but create nothing. And that is why we are *bhogis*. Scientists have tried to duplicate a thought impulse through chemical activity, and they had to spend a million dollars to create a thought impulse in the laboratory. If it is thirty crores of rupees or approximately 8.5 million dollars for one thought, how many thoughts could you entertain everyday? And you say that you are a poor man! But, in fact, you are so rich – creating thoughts that are very costly.

God creates everything with almost nothing. That is His creativity! That is His ingenuity! Earth comes from water. From where does water come? Water comes from fire. If you separate a water molecule by electrolysis, it separates into hydrogen and oxygen atoms. Hydrogen is an inflammable gas, and oxygen helps ignite it. From where does fire come? Fire comes from air. Without air there cannot be any fire. From where does air come? Air is nothing but movement in space. If there is no space, there can't be any movement. Ultimately, we are nothing but space. The *rishis* discovered that. Take an atom of which your cells are made, of which your tissues are made, of which your whole system is made. An atom is 99.99 per cent space, that is, the primary space. From space everything is born. For the scientist, the elemental constituents of matter are the proton, electron and neutron. For the *rishi*, the elemental constituents are *sattva*, *rajas* and *tamas*. The electron goes around the nucleus that consists of the proton and neutron. *Sattva* and *tamas* remain together. They look alike, also. Both the *tamasic* and *sattvic* persons are quiet. But one person is quietly sleeping, while the other's mind is trying to embrace the whole universe. That is the difference between a *tamasic* and *sattvic* person. In *tamas* there is no activity but only darkness. In *sattva* there is no activity but, rather, a quiet alertness. The *sattvic* person is full of light while the *rajasic* person moves around. The whole thing is spinning in space. Space is an evolute of these *gunas*. *Sattva*, *rajas* and *tamas* evolve as space. *Sattva*, *rajas* and *tamas* are three streams of the modification of energy. *Sakti* modifies as *sattva*, *rajas* and *tamas*. *Sakti* belongs to the *Sakta*, to *Siva*. *Siva* is *Sakta* because he has *Sakti*. *Siva* is the ultimate truth, the reality. So everything can be folded back into *Siva*; and that *Siva* is your root, your true nature. When you unfold and finally dissolve into *Siva*, that state of *Sakti* uniting with *Siva* is the state of illumination and final fulfillment.

The process of uplifting *Sakti*, and uniting with *Siva* – called

Sivasaktisamyoga – is to lift ourselves from our present entanglement and then unite with *Siva*. In other words you can say, "*Jiva Brahmaaikya.*" In *Sivasaktisamyoga* there is total bliss. The whole cosmos becomes a celebration. Millions of suns and stars appear in that state of *Sivasaktisamyoga*.

Sakti has three manifestations – *iccha sakti, kriya sakti* and *jnana sakti*. For any creation you need these three powers, otherwise, creation is not possible. Suppose we want to build a house. The first thing needed is *jnana sakti*. One should first *know* the process of building a house. Next one needs *iccha sakti* or the capacity to make up one's mind. Generally, we don't firm up our minds. Our minds constantly change. The capacity to take a resolve, a decision, and stick to that decision and channelize your entire energy for the fulfillment of your decision is *iccha sakti*. Many times we lack that power – *arambhasurah khalu bharatiyah* – our resolve fades. Initially, we are very enthusiastic; we think we will do it. After some time we say, "I don't think I will be able to do it after all." We start thinking of obstacles. We don't have the resolve and will power. We lack the power of sustained enthusiasm.

To create we need knowledge – *jnana sakti*, as well as *iccha sakti* or will power, and then we need *kriya sakti* – the technology or the skill. Mere knowledge is insufficient. We might explain to everyone how to ride a cycle: "First, sit on the cycle; balance yourself on the bike; rotate the pedals with your feet; and when the back wheel moves, the front wheel will also move." It is very easy to explain. Then, ask a person to ride a cycle. He will be powerless to move! The knowledge has not yet unfolded as a skill. We may have the knowledge, but we lack the skill. Skill comes out of habit. The repeated exercising of knowledge produces skill. Expertise comes from repeatedly using one's knowledge in different ways.

For creation *iccha sakti, jnana sakti* and *kriya sakti* are necessary. And *sakti* has all these aspects of power. *Sakti* has *iccha sakti*. She has *jnana sakti*. And she has *kriya sakti*, too. *Sakti* comes down first as *akasa*, then *vayu*, *agni*, *apa* and, finally, *prthvi*. *Sakti* evolves, and finally it comes to identify with the individuated, particularized aspect of existence – this individualized body-mind. And, even as a particular body-mind, we are identified with *kama*, *krodha* and *lobha*. These are our identifications. *Kama* is desire for food and procreation. These are two dominant desires of humankind. First, we want to preserve this body. For that, food is necessary. We also want to preserve our race. For that, procreation is necessary. *Kama* is the basic driving force in an ordinary individual. He is not able to lift himself above that level. When we sit down quietly and analyze, what is the dominating force in us? It is *kama*. Let us accept that fact.

When that desire is not fulfilled, then we experience *krodha* (anger). If the desire is fulfilled, then there is a craving for repetition – *lobha*. Once our desire is fulfilled, we want a repetition of that. Once we visit Goa and enjoy the place, again we want to go there. We want to repeat the same experience.

The *Sakti* identified with the body-mind is under the influence of these three modes of matter – ***kama, krodha*** and ***lobha***. This is where we are. The ***Bhagavad Gita*** says, "***trividham narakasyedam dvaram (XVI.xxi)***." "There are three gates to hell" – ***kama, krodha*** and ***lobha***.

The infinite creative power of *Siva* – so much identified with the limited equipment, remaining in two-and-a-half coils at the root of the personality – is known as ***kundalini sakti***. It is "***kundalam***" because it is coiled. She is curled up in a ***kundala*** form. She has no expression. It is like potential energy that has not become kinetic; it has not become activated. Until Hanumanji met Sri Ram, Hanumanji's ***kundalini*** was not awakened. Hanumanji was the unemployed minister of an unemployed king. If the managing director is unemployed, his secretary will also be unemployed. Once he met Ram, at the very sight of Ram, Hanumanji experienced the awakening of his inner power. When Mahatma Gandhi went to Africa, he was unable to even express himself in the court while presenting his case. His ***kundalini*** was dormant. But once he was enraptured by the idea of independence, freedom for his people, his ***kundalini*** started awakening.

This power which remains latent – which remains in a state of potency *in* you, that power has to be awakened! Its full potential has to be utilized. Finally, it has to be mingled with Consciousness – Lord Siva, so that one's life becomes a cosmic dance – an *utsav*, a celebration. This is the ultimate purpose of life.

Where is the identification of *kundalini* now? The place in which the *kundalini* is lying, unconscious, in deep slumber is called the *muladhara cakra*. The *muladhara* lies at the base of one's spinal column. *Kundalini sakti* is lying in the *muladhara*, unconscious, in deep slumber, unaware of its powers. We have to *awaken* the *kundalini* from the *muladhara*.

The *Kundalini Shastra* discusses seven *cakras*. According to the *Shastras*, the human being is the centre of the universe. I don't know whether you will agree with that statement or not, but according to the *Kundalini Shastra* you are the centre of the universe. If someone asks you, "What is the centre of the universe?" you reply, "How do I know? I am standing here. The universe extends on all sides. How do I know where the centre of universe is? I have no method of measuring the universe." But one witty Hindu said, "I am the centre of universe. If you want, you can disprove me. I am the centre of the universe because the universe is presented to me. The universe is impinging upon me from all sides." It is like a wheel revolving round a hub. When I say, "I am the centre of the universe," I don't mean that this body is the centre of the universe. I mean that the light of Consciousness in me, which makes me aware of my thoughts, my body and the world outside, is the centre of the universe. Let's appreciate this fact.

Unfortunately, we don't know this fact. We identify with

limited things in the universe. Hence, we have become ignorant people. Ignorance means ignoring the total and identifying with the particular, seeing the tree and missing the forest. We miss the forest because of the tree. Some people miss the tree because of the forest. That also is wrong. We must be able to see the particular tree in the context of the totality of trees. We must be able to experience ourselves as part of the totality. Thus we transcend all limitations.

Presently your *kundalini* is dormant, and this means you are under the influence of *kama, krodha* and *lobha*. As long as we are under that influence, always thinking of eating and procreating – which we are doing gladly and cheerfully – there is no hope of uniting with *Siva*. So now, what should we do?

To begin with, one needs to practise three values. No spiritual practice is possible without a certain ethical discipline. Let me be very clear: Some people say, "You can smoke, drink or do anything. But chant this *mantra*, and then give me three hundred dollars and things will be all right." Such advice is indecent; it is more haste to acquire dollars rather than to improve the aspirant. One must practise three values. The three values are encapsulated in the syllables, *da-da-da*, which Brahmaji taught. *Da* means *dama, daya* and *dana*. If you want to be a spiritual person these three values are to be practised.

Dama means discipline, austerity. Reduce your needs. Instead of *kama*, practice *dama*. To counteract *krodha* you have to practice *daya*. Some of the *gurus* instruct, "Whenever you come to me, bring a flower. Take your ego and put it in that flower." It is a symbolic gesture. Offering a flower to the *guru* means you are offering your ego, because the flower has fragrance, beauty and a vanity of its own – even if it is only for a few hours before it fades away. Of course, this is only a symbolic gesture, and it is not that you can pluck your ego and put it in a flower and give it to the *guru*. It is a gesture that creates a culture. The culture creates an attitude. Over a period of time you will be able to live it.

Kama is to be eliminated by discipline and austerity. *Krodha* is to be disciplined by *daya*, the act of compassion and forgiveness. Forgiveness and patience are very important even in our daily practical life. People do make mistakes. One has to forgive them. You yourself make mistakes. Unless you forgive, you will be caught up in the past. You will not be able to liberate yourself from the past.

Lobha is to be eliminated by *dana*. Develop the practice of sharing and giving. *Dama, daya* and *dana* are the three values to be practised as an initial step to deeper spirituality.

The *rishis* have said that there is a subtle, invisible *nadi*, known as the *atmanadi*, among the 727,210,201 *nadis* through which our life juices flow and make us alive. It is an invisible passage through which Consciousness flows into the system. A *nadi*, according to the *rishis*, is one millionth the size of a human hair. That is why every pick of a needle gives us pain – the life juices reach every portion of the body, even space as infinitesmal as a needle point! Medical science has not been able to discover this fact of Consciousness.

There is another *nadi* called the *sushumna*. This *nadi*, which runs from the brain to the root of the spine, almost touching the anus, is very vital in *sadhana*. It is through that *nadi* that the sleeping energy has to be awakened. Finally, *Sakti* has to reach the *sahasrara*, the seat of *Siva*. The *sahasrara* is constantly nourished by Consciousness through the *atmanadi*. The separation of *Sakti* from *Siva* is the cause of all our miseries. When we separate the child from its mother, the child is in misery; the beloved separated from the lover, is in misery. In union there is bliss. In disunion there is misery. *Sakti* has to be united with *Siva*. One has to merge with Supreme Consciousness.

Now *Sakti* is rooted in the *muladhara* at the base of the spinal column, from where we have to lift this energy. *Sakti* remains covered by *bhutattva*, and the quality of *bhutattva* is fragrance. How does the doctor administer the anesthesia? Fragrance has a great power to hypnotize us. *Sakti* is overpowered by *bhutattva*. That is the quality of the *muladhara*. The *sushumna* is blocked by *bhutattva*.

Visualize all this. Please don't ask me whether I can medically prove all these things. Unfortunately, ninety per cent of the Truth cannot be proven medically. Neither can ninety per cent of existence be proven medically. It is something like trying to measure the water of the ocean spoon by spoon. There are people like that who go to the ocean with a spoon. They make a small ditch somewhere on the shore, rush to the ocean, take a spoonful of water, rush back to the ditch and pour it there. Will they ever be able to measure the ocean? With our limited spoon, the brain and our ratiocinating, our logical thinking, we are unable to measure existence. Existence cannot be measured by simple thinking. We have to use an entire repertoire of faculties to measure the depth and variety of existence. We have to use intuition, surrender and devotion. Numerous instruments are to be developed and then used for understanding. Otherwise the mystery of existence will not be grasped.

Above the *muladhara* is the *svadhisthan*, the seat of *jalatattva*. Above the *svadhisthan* is the *manipura cakra*. It is almost on the side of the navel. *Manipura* is a major nerve centre. If a karate expert should just jab the navel of the opponent there, his opponent is finished. He knows how to affect the vital nerve. He doesn't have to punch or hit. *Manipura* is the seat of *agnitattva* – fire. Above the *manipura*, near the heart, is the *anahata cakra*. *Anahata cakra* is the seat of *vayu*. Above the *anahata* near the throat is *visuddha cakra*. *Visuddha cakra* is the seat of *akasatattva*.

Two inches above the *muladhara-bhutattva* is the *svadhisthan-jalatattva*. Two inches above *svadhisthan* on the navel is *manipura-agnitattva*. Above the *manipura-agnitattva*, in the region of the heart, is *anahata-vayutattva*. In the region of the throat is *visuddha-akasatattva*. Above the *visuddha cakra*, between the eyebrows, is the *ajna cakra*, the seat of *triguna* in the form of *Sakti*. Above the *ajna cakra* is the *sahasrara*, the seat of *Siva*.

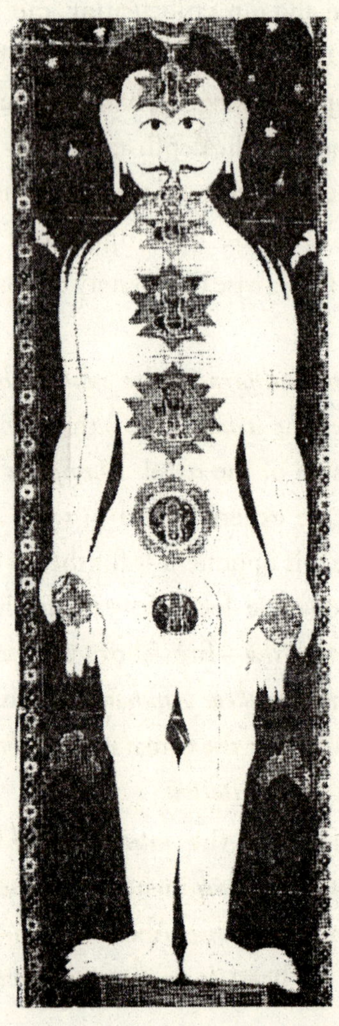

Each *cakra* has a different number of petals or spokes. The *muladhara* has four petals. *Svadhisthan* has six, and the *manipura* has ten petals. *Anahata* has twelve petals. *Visuddha* has sixteen petals, and the *ajna cakra* has only two petals. Why two petals? Because here the diversity is being reduced to just the fundamental duality. Beyond the *ajna cakra* is the *sahasrara*, the land of infinitude. It is the land of a million lotuses ever in full bloom.

The *sadhaka* needs to have some techniques of awakening this power through the *sushumna* – the subtle *nadi* – and come to be united with *Siva*. Thereafter, he or she will experience everything as the dance of *Siva*, the manifestation of *Siva*. This is the *Siva-Sakti Tandava*.

How do you get that experience? A simple technique is chanting *Aum* while focusing your attention on each *cakra*. With your mouth closed, take a deep breath through both the nostrils while seated in *sukhasana*. Instead of focusing on the *bhrumadhya*, focus on the *muladhara*, at the root of the spinal column. Then take another deep breath. Hold that breath inside as long as possible. Then release the breath *through the mouth*. While taking a breath, chant *Aum*. While you hold the breath, chant *Aum* mentally. When you release the breath, also chant *Aum* loudly. As you take a breath, synchronize it with *Aum*. Keep your attention on the *muladhara*. Practice this for a minimum of three days for forty-five minutes each day.

For the next three days concentrate on the *svadhisthan*, the six-petaled lotus two inches above *muladhara,* and then repeat the entire process.

Thus, until the *ajna cakra*, you have to chant *Aum*. You will find the *sushumna* opening and energy going up. Your body will shake, and you may hear various sounds.

Just now, I will not explain all the things that you will see. If I mention these to you without anything really happening, you may begin to imagine these experiences. With real practice, you will hear celestial music, divine sounds, notice divine fragrances – *alaukika sabda, alaukika gandha* – hear waterfalls, see flowers falling. In the *Ramayana* there is a beautiful description of flowers falling continuously, making a trail touching both heaven and earth. Narayana *Guru* talks about a million black cobras simultaneously raising their hoods. In the *Bhagavad Gita* it is said, *divi surya sahasrasya... bhasas tasya mahatmanah (XI.xii)* – "a thousand suns simultaneously arise."

As the power goes to the *sahasrara*, you start getting very powerful hints or suggestions and experiences. As the *kundalini* breaks open, the *cakras* bloom, manifesting their *gunas* in full form. The *bhutattva* manifests the *guna* of fragrance. The *aptattva* manifests the *guna* of taste – without eating you will start tasting heavenly dishes. The *agnitattva* manifests the *guna* of color. Rainbows continuously appear. This *sadhana* is very powerful; hence, you must be very careful. When the *vayutattva* manifests, you will feel as if you are being tickled by millions of peacock feathers. Every cell is tickled by a divine touch. As it comes to the *ajna cakra*, the *akasatattva* manifests. Various sounds are heard, the so-called "music of the spheres."

When it comes to the *ajna cakra*, you experience great silence and peace. The *utsav* – the celebration or festival – is over. There is a deep sense of satiation, and most people get stuck there.

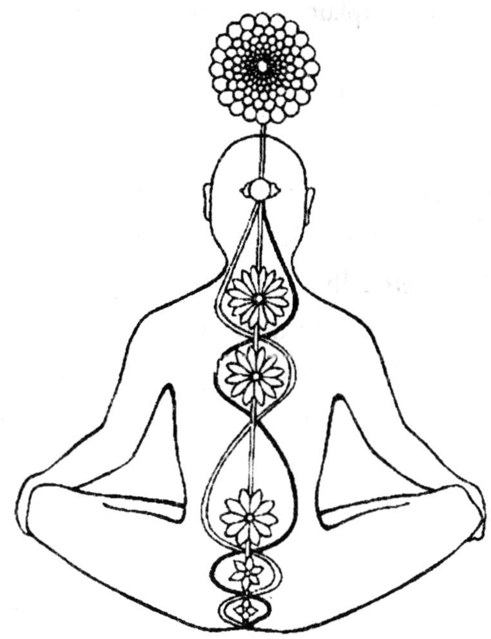

For lifting your *kundalini* to *Siva*, you have to chant the *Soham mantra*. So from *Aum* you shift to *Soham*, using the same process: chant the *Soham mantra* for forty-five minutes, fixing your attention between the eyebrows. Chant "*Soham*" and dissolve in *Siva*. When the energy falls into *Siva*, into the embrace of *Siva*, *Siva* is aroused. Without *Sakti*, *Siva* remains quiet. Once *Sakti* unites with *Siva,* then the whole universe blooms in myriad forms of color, touch, taste, smell – your experience will be beyond description.

This is one form of meditation – of awakening your inner potential. A person who has awakened can never be tired thereafter. He is always inspired. He has plenty of energy. Whatever he touches turns into gold. He becomes the most creative person. The *kundalini* power, disunited from *Siva,* because of its slumber, remains identified with limited, enclosed matter. That is "the fall." In the Bible the fall of man is described. In *our* scriptures we talk about another kind of fall of man. Finally, the "fallen man" has to awaken to his full potential. That is possible by means of this *kundalini* meditation. Once it is awakened, there is total satisfaction for the meditator.

Meditation on Cosmic Power

Asana and *Pranayama*: Sit in *sukhasana* with your legs interlocked and your hands resting on the knees. Your mental attention is between the eyebrows and follows the breath, the in-going and out-going breath. Feel that you are just the breath:

"I am the breath – when the breath goes out, I go out."

Mingle with the *samasti prana*.

"When the breath comes in, I come in. I am not the body – I am the breath."

One who identifies with the body is a *jantu* – *jayate mriyate iti jantu*. "I am not a *jantu*; I am a *prani*."

Prana is the root of the psycho-physical complex. Realize the fact that you are the *prana*, the vital air. Don't slouch. Sit straight and experience the *pranic* energy. Think, "I am the *prana*. It is this *prana* that governs my thoughts, my physiological activities and physical activities. And as the *prana* that I am, I go out and come in." Look upon the *prana* as the manifestation of the Lord.

To help the process of watching, breathe deeply and deliberately. Breathe in slowly, and breathe out slowly, deliberately and deeply.

Watch the breath going out and coming in.

When we watch the body, we feel that it is an object of our experience. In this state we may experience sensations but we are not disturbed. There are no disturbances whatsoever. Keep your eyes closed throughout the meditation session; then alone can you develop trust in the Lord. Remain in *sukhasana* breathing deeply, deliberately and slowly. With great devotion breathe in and breathe out. You feel cool.

We begin the chanting of *Aum*: First I will chant and then you please follow.

When chanting on your own, begin with three *Aums*:

Aum ... (group chanting)
Aum ... (group chanting)
Aum ... (group chanting)

Mudra Practice

Next we practise the *mudras* without chanting the *mantra*. I will guide you, so don't do these on your own at this time. First, there will be an instruction, and then please follow it. Don't anticipate any command. When the command comes to you, then follow it. An anticipating mind falls prey to tension and excitement. In meditation we want to reduce the level of tension. Tension is the cause of many modern diseases, so don't anticipate the command. When you are in a posture, be in that posture, totally and completely. When the next command comes, then flow into that posture. Thus you will learn how to discipline the mind.

With your hands in *sukha mudra*, your palms resting on your knees, bring your attention to the *prana*. As you observe your breath, you feel very light, very serene. You feel that you are the *prana* rather than the body. As you identify more and more with the *prana*, a new light develops inside. You feel your whole existence has become illuminated, full of light and bliss and coolness, and you experience a total sense of leisure.

Without opening your eyes, raise your hands – palms together – to the level of the heart into the *bhakti mudra*, slowly and gracefully like the opening of a flower. You are building up certain spiritual energy; by opening your eyes you dissipate this energy. Breathe deeply and deliberately. When you are breathing in, you are breathing in the entire cosmos because the same *prana* is one everywhere.

Now lift your hands over your head slowly and gracefully. Stretch your muscles. Let your whole body become like a flame. Let all the three hundred billion cells in the body flow upwards. Now you are sitting like a pyramid. A pyramid is a great energy centre, like a mountain peak. As Trisanku says in the Vedas, "I have become the highest mountain peak." Feel that you have really become a flame, a mountain peak. Supplicate to the Universal Mother. You own nothing. You have nothing. You are evaporated into Cosmic Consciousness.

Slowly open your hands towards the sky in a surge of upward energy, flying into eternity.

Now let your hands rest on your knees, palms upward with your thumb and forefinger touching, in *jnana mudra.*

Concentrate on the *prana.* Breathe deeply while keeping your eyes closed.

Now bring your left hand towards the navel, and place your right hand on the left hand. Sit like a Buddha. Your attention is on the *prana.* Breathe deeply, deliberately. Let the whole body participate in breathing.

Now bring your hands up to the chest. With your right hand in a fist and the thumb protruding upward, place your right hand on top of your left palm. Tilt your chin upwards a little, and, keeping your eyes closed, breathe deeply.

Slowly hold your palms out, receptively, in *prasada mudra.* Feel the blessings of the Universal Mother. Feel Her blessings enveloping you totally and passing into you.

Again move your hands back into *bhakti mudra*, pressing your palms together.

Now slowly drop your hands back onto your knees – slowly, without any haste – and smile without parting the lips.

Without opening your eyes, let us do some stretching exercises. Stretch in any manner you want, but don't move from your original place. Do this with your eyes closed. You are not allowed to scratch. Stretch your legs, hands, neck. Stretch slowly. Exercise your neck by rotating it slowly clockwise – forward, sideways, back, to the side, and forward once again, without opening your eyes.

Now come back to your original position.

Sit in *sukhasana*. Practise *pranayama*. Block your left nostril with the ring finger of your right hand, breathe in through the right nostril. Fill your lungs with fresh *prana*. Now block both the nostrils, and sit in *antakumbhaka*, retaining the breath for as long as you can. Then release air through the left nostril. Practise this six times.

Now stop *pranayama*, and sit in *sukhasana* with your body erect, your attention between the eyebrows, observing the in-going and out-going breath. Feel the energy coming; feel all your *nadis* overflowing with energy. Feel the descent of the Universal Mother into your life. She is dancing in your system. Feel that ecstasy of being close to Universal Mother. All your *nadis* are thrilled. With her touch every cell is alive. Feel....

Mudra and Mantra Together

Next we perform all the *mudras* along with a *mantra*. Please listen while I chant the *mantra*. Then repeat the *mantra* after listening to the chant:

Aum... hreem... kleem... svaha (group chanting)
Aum... hreem... kleem... svaha (group chanting)
Aum... hreem... kleem... svaha (group chanting)
Aum... hreem... kleem... svaha (group chanting)
Aum... hreem... kleem... svaha (group chanting)
Aum... hreem... kleem... svaha (group chanting)
Aum... hreem... kleem... svaha (group chanting)

Now bring your hands together into *bhakti mudra*, and slowly take a deep breath:

Aum... hreem... kleem... svaha (group chanting)
Aum... hreem... kleem... svaha (group chanting)
Aum... hreem... kleem... svaha (group chanting)

Now lift your hands up to steeple form in *saranagati mudra*. Stretch your muscles. Become a flame:

Aum... hreem... kleem... svaha (group chanting)
Aum... hreem... kleem... svaha (group chanting)
Aum... hreem... kleem... svaha (group chanting)

Now open your hands and stretch them towards the sky in *prapatti mudra*. As you do this, tilt your chin slightly upwards:

Aum... hreem... kleem... svaha (group chanting)
Aum... hreem... kleem... svaha (group chanting)

Now drop your hands on to your knees, palms upward with your thumb and forefinger touching, in *jnana mudra.* Take a long deep breath. Feel that energy within you. Feel the overflowing ecstasy in every cell, the abundance of Mother's blessings. You feel exhilarated. The light fills you like a flood – you feel uplifted. The body is no more a weight, a burden:

Aum... hreem... kleem... svaha (group chanting)
Aum... hreem... kleem... svaha (group chanting)
Aum... hreem... kleem... svaha (group chanting)

Bring your left hand to the navel with the right hand placed on top of it in *dhyana mudra*. Press your navel a little and sit up straight keeping your eyes closed. Bring your attention to the point between the eyebrows. Now you are just the *prana*:

Aum... hreem... kleem... svaha (group chanting)
Aum... hreem... kleem... svaha (group chanting)
Aum... hreem... kleem... svaha (group chanting)

Bring your hands to the chest and heart region in *yoga mudra*. Make a fist with your right hand and place it upon the left hand. The thumb of your right hand should protrude upward:

Aum... hreem... kleem... svaha (group chanting)
Aum... hreem... kleem... svaha (group chanting)
Aum... hreem... kleem... svaha (group chanting)

Now hold your hands out in *prasada mudra*. Feel the cool

sensation coming in, the blessing of Universal Mother – *Jagat Janani*:

Aum... hreem... kleem... svaha (group chanting)
Aum... hreem... kleem... svaha (group chanting)
Aum... hreem... kleem... svaha (group chanting)

Bring your hands together to *bhakti mudra*:

Aum... hreem... kleem... svaha (group chanting)
Aum... hreem... kleem... svaha (group chanting)
Aum... hreem... kleem... svaha (group chanting)

Drop the palms of your hands onto the knees in *ananda mudra*. Take a long, deep breath. Smile without parting the lips.

The Mother is going through all your veins from all sides. In sheer pure ecstasy, feel the *mantra*:

Aum... hreem... kleem... svaha (group chanting)
Aum... hreem... kleem... svaha (group chanting)
Aum... hreem... kleem... svaha (group chanting)

Visualize the *jyoti* of the Universal Mother. Visualize Her manifesting as the brilliance of a thousand shining Suns in dazzling brilliance – the golden brilliance of the Universal Mother.

See Her:

Aum... hreem... kleem... svaha (group chanting)
Aum... hreem... kleem... svaha (group chanting)
Aum... hreem... kleem... svaha (group chanting)

Purnamada purnamidam
purnat purnamudacyate
purnasya purnamadaya
purnamevavasisyate
Aum Santih Santih Santih

(*Brhadaranyaka* & *Isa Upanishad,* Invocation)

Aum sarve bhavantu sukhinah
sarve santu niramayah
sarve bhadrani pasyantu
ma kaschit duhkhabhag bhavet
Aum Santih Santih Santih

(Ancient Sanskrit Prayer)

Aum asato ma sadgamaya
tamaso ma jyotirgamaya
mrtyorma amrtam gamaya
Aum Santih Santih Santih

(Brhadaranyaka Upanishad, I.iii.xxviii)

Slowly open your eyes and unlock your legs.

Go.

Go with this precious gift you have received.

GLOSSARY

adbhya prthvi – *Ap* and *prthvi* are two of the five primary elements. *Prthvi*, the earth element, emerges from *adbhya*, the water element. *Adbhya* is the declined form of *ap*. (See *Taittitriya Upanishad* II.1)

agnitattva – The idea that the microcosm is the centre of the macrocosm is a unique concept in the Hindu *Tantra Sastra*. Each *cakra* is the seat of one of the five elements. Thus, *agnitattva*, the fire element, is situated in the *manipura*, the third *cakra*.

ahimsa – Variously defined as non-harmfulness or non-violence; love or respect for the uniqueness of the other or for all creatures; accommodation; non-reaction or non-exploitation. One of the five great values Patanjali prescribes for *yoga*. (See *yama*)

ajna – According to *kundalini yoga* philosophy, the sixth spiritual centre of human personality situated between the brows. (See *cakra*)

akasatattva – The first of the five primary elements which make up the universe. In the microcosm, *akasatattva* is situated in the *visuddhi cakra*, the throat region. (See *cakra*)

alaukika gandha – Smell experienced by the inner sense of an awakened *yogi* – transcendental smell.

alaukika sabda – The sound which is not cognized by physical sense organs but heard by the inner sense of an awakened *yogi* whose *visuddhi cakra* is activated by the aroused *kundalini*.

anahata – The fourth *cakra*, situated in the heart region. (See *cakra*)

ananda – Literally, bliss; the nature of *Brahman*. In this context, it refers to a *mudra*, a gesture indicating bliss. (See *mudra*)

annat purusha – *Purusha* means the body-mind which is born of modifications of *anna*; *annat* is the declined form of the word, *anna*, and means food.

antacaksu – The inner eye which is opened in an accomplished *yogi*.

antahkarana – The inner equipment consisting of mind (*manah*), intellect (*buddhi*), ego (*ahamkara*) and memory (*citta*), which are the instruments of receiving, processing and responding to sensations.

antakumbhaka – Holding the breath inside. There are four limbs of *pranayama*. The first limb of *pranayama* is inhaling; the second is pausing or retaining the breath; third, exhaling; fourth, again pausing; and, finally, inhaling again. (See *pranayama*)

antara – Means "inner." Refers to *samadhi* attained by meditating on a mental image. (See *samadhi*)

antara drsyanuviddha – Seeing all thought modifications as the play of Consciousness by knowing that all thoughts are only changing names and forms. *Drgdrsyaviveka* 23-25.

antara sabdanuviddha – *Samadhi* attained by the aid of words or sounds that remind one of the Self. Gaining Self-abidance with the help of "silent" chanting and reflection upon *mantras* such as *Aum* or *Shivoham,* or by seeing that all thought modifications are the play of Consciousness. *Drgdrsyaviveka* 23-25. (See *samadhi*)

antasitalata – The experience of inner quietude or of coolness in *samadhi.*

anudata – Modulation of the pitch in chanting a *mantra.*

anugraha – The blessings or benediction bestowed by a deity upon a devotee.

aparigraham – Non-possessiveness; one of the five great values Patanjali prescribes for a seeker.

"*Arambhasurah khalu bharatiyah*" – A common Indian saying meaning that Indians show only initial enthusiasm in any endeavour but easily wear out. Perhaps the reason for such an attitude is the heat of the sub-continental summer, the other-worldliness of the people, their tendency to explain a problem in terms of the past rather than solving it by innovative behaviour, or the sheer chaos and disorder of the society.

ardhanilimitam – *Ardha* means "half," and *nilimitam* means "closed eyes." In meditation, with half-closed eyes, one looks at the tip of the nose to avoid sleep and to focus attention away from sensory distractions.

arjavam – Straightforwardness, integrity. According to the

Bhagavad Gita, one of the twenty qualities necessary for a seeker. *Gita* XIII.7.

arohana – Means the ascending or rising pitch. In chanting *Om*/*Aum*, one starts in a low pitch and raises this pitch in the middle of *AUM*. This helps to draw the sound from the very depth of the stomach. (See A*um*)

asamprajnata – *Samprajna* means "with consciousness," and *a* means "absence of." A state of consciousness free from a sense of separation and the egoistic notions of *I* and *mine*. A state of effortless watchfulness detached from thoughts and sensations and characterized by identification with the light of Consciousness. This state is gained by knowledge of the Self, by devotion, and through psychic disciplines like breath control and inner absorption. (See *samadhi*) *Yoga Sutras* I.18.

asana – A particular posture used during meditation. Also a mat used for sitting during meditation. "*Sthirasukhamasanam*" – a steady, comfortable posture – Patanjali defines *asana* as the third stage of *yogic* discipline. *Yoga Sutras* II.46.

ashram – A place of rest and renewal where renunciants live – in the forest, on riverbanks, away from the city, living a life of austerity, prayer and meditation. Also, a place where students and disciples gather.

ashtanga yoga – This is the eight-fold path of *yoga* prescribed by Patanjali (*Yoga Sutras* II.29). They are: public values, personal disciplines, postures, breathing exercises, detachment, refocusing the mind on the inner Self, abiding in the Self, and identity with the Self.

asteyam – Non-stealing. Austere, simple lifestyle; sharing. One of the five great virtues prescribed by Patanjali for a spiritual seeker. *Yoga Sutras* II.30.

"atha yoganusasanam" – "Now/Thereafter, instructions in *yoga*;" the first *sutra* of Patanjali's *Yoga Sutras* I.1.

atmanadi – The channel through which Universal Consciousness flows into the *sahasrara,* the highest evolutionary point of individual energy, or the seat of Supreme Bliss. *Ramana Gita* IX.10; V.5-6. (See *cakra*)

Aum/Om – The vibration in timeless Consciousness that manifests as the universe. The three syllables of *Om* – A-U-M, represent the waking, dream, and sleep states of consciousness. The silence underlying *Om* vibrations represent pure consciousness. The chanting of *Om* is the method of awakening the individual consciousness from ego limitations to its full potential of infinitude.

avarohana – The descending pitch, for example, in which the chanting of *Om* ends. (See *Aum*)

bahya – Outer. (See *samadhi*)

bahyacakshu – Literally, the external eye, but it can refer to any of the five sense organs.

bahya drsyanuviddha – Spiritual absorption or abiding in timeless Consciousness with the aid of external objects; a subjective understanding that one is the light of Consciousness illumining external cognition. Seeing the play of Consciousness everywhere in the outer world by knowing the falsity of the names and forms that disguise the Truth. *Drgdrsyaviveka* 23-25. (See *samadhi*)

bahyakumbhaka – Retention of the breath outside after exhaling. (See *pranayama*)

bahya sabdanuviddha – Spiritual absorption or abiding in timeless Consciousness with the aid of a word like "*Om*" or "*Siva*" or a phrase such as "I am infinite Bliss; all that I experience is verily an expression of *Brahman*." The meditation gained by following the meaning of these *mantras* and seeing the play of Consciousness in every external object with the help of *mantra*. *Drgdrsyaviveka* 23-25. (See *samadhi*)

Bhagavad Gita – One of the three holy books of Hinduism. Part of the great epic, *Mahabharata*, Chapters 25-43 of the *Bhishma Parva*, consisting of a spiritual dialogue between Sri Krishna, the Hindu god, and Arjuna, the Hindu warrior prince. This dialogue takes place in the midst of the battlefield, Kurukshetra, as the Pandava and Kaurava armies face one another. It is an impassioned exhortation to do one's duty as an offering to God, without reacting to the fruits thereof. Through the means of following the path known as Karma Yoga, Bhakti is developed, and through Bhakti comes the final reward of living in eternal God-Consciousness also known as Gyana Yoga.

Bhagavan – Usually, God, who enjoys *bhaga* – glories like omniscience, omnipresence and sovereignty, etc. It is also a prefix used for anyone with extraordinary spiritual powers, i.e. *Bhagavan* Sankara, *Bhagavan* Patanjali, *Bhagavan* Vyasa, etc.

bhakti – Devotion to God; living in spiritual consciousness; love for all – the same attitude can be invoked with the help of a gesture, in this case, the palms held together in adoration – the common gesture with which Indians greet one another, especially honored souls. (See *mudra*)

bhava – A generic term denoting a higher state of mind – like devotion, knowledge, ecstasy, absorption, purity, or compassion.

bodha – (See *mudra*)

bhogi – Indulgent; one who thinks that sense pleasures are the ultimate objective of life.

bhrumadhya – The point between the eyebrows; the seat of the *ajna cakra*, the last frontier before the *sahasrara*, the land of bliss.

bhutattva – The earth element situated in the *muladhara cakra,* the first spiritual centre, which is located in the anal region where *kundalini* sleeps in two-and-a-half coils. (See *cakra*)

brahmacharya – The discipline for attaining *Brahman*, Supreme Bliss; that which takes one to God, living in God, and love for God; the practice of continence or celibacy for the purpose of preserving one's vital energy for the awakening of *kundalini*, the final union with *Siva* or Bliss. *Brahmacharayam* is the discipline of *brahmacharya* itself.

Brahmaji – The four-headed Creator of the universe who sits in a lotus that grows from the navel of *Vishnu*; one among the triad of Hindu deities. The timeless *Brahman* expressing as the creative power; the highest point of the ego's evolution. One aspect of *Brahman's* manifestation that lives for 100 Divine years or 4.3 million x 1000 x 2 x 365 x 100 human years. *Bhagavad Gita* VIII.17.

Brahman – The Supreme Truth: Existence, Knowledge, Bliss; Timeless, Space-less, Division-less, Quality-less Silence; the Supreme Cause of everything; Non-changing, Non-evolving Eternity to be realized by the *yogi* as the Innermost Self.

Brahmasutras – One of the three holy books of Hinduism. A logical and persuasive exegesis which establishes the purport of the *Upanishads* as revealing the unity of the individual soul with the Universal Spirit, or, put another way, of the soul as the expression of the Universal Spirit. The *Upanishads* are the revealed wisdom of Hindu tradition in the form of *mantras* or hymns. The *Brahmasutras* are divided into four chapters and have 534 aphorisms. Sri Veda Vyasa Badarayana is considered to be the author. These *sutras* are generally read along with the commentary of Sankaracharya, A.D. 788-820. (See *Vyasa*)

buddhi – Intellect. The discriminating, deliberating, reasoning and deciding faculty of the inner organ comprised of *manah* (feeling), *buddhi* (intellect), *ahamkara* (ego) and *citta* (memories). (See *antahkarana*)

caitanya – The Supreme Truth which is boundless Consciousness and bliss, otherwise called *atman*, *Brahman*, *pratyagatman*, etc.

Turiya Caitanya	Jagrat	Swapna	Susupti
Consciousness	Conscious	Subconsciousness	Unconscious
	Waker	Dreamer	Sleeper

cakra – The psychic centres discussed in *Kundalini Sastra*. The *cakras* are: *muladhara, svadhisthana, manipura, anahata, visuddhi, ajna, sahasrara*. They are also called lotuses: the anal lotus, generative lotus, navel lotus, heart lotus, throat lotus, eye lotus, and bliss lotus.

chandan – Sandal paste, applied to the forehead of a devotee, especially by the devotees of *Vishnu*, one of the triad of Hindu gods. Sandal paste, being cool and fragrant, has the power to activate neurotransmitters helpful to uplift one's mood and make the mind quiet and alert.

citta – Memories. (See *antahkarana*)

cittasya desa bandhata – Focusing mind upon a chosen, limited space; concentration practices in *yoga* discipline. One can choose to concentrate on a form or a sound, mental or external. (See *dharana*) *Yoga Sutras* III.1.

Dakshinamurti Stotram – Sri Sankaracharya composed this hymn of 10 verses unto Lord Dakshinamurti, who, in order to teach his devotees, appeared as an incarnation of Lord Shiva in the form of a *guru*. Lord Dakshinamurti is considered the first *guru* of the Vedantic tradition. Though purported to be a hymn of adoration, it is one of the finest and clearest expositions of the Vedantic vision of Oneness.

dama, daya, dana – Austerity, compassion, sharing – indicated through the syllables "*da, da, da.*" The story goes that humans, gods and demons for instruction approached Prajapati. He uttered these three syllables and disappeared. The indulgent gods needed the restraint of austerity; the greedy humans had need for charity or sharing; and the demons needed to curb their cruelty with compassion. To survive, the modern human needs all the three values in abundant measure. T.S. Eliot quotes this *Upanishadic* statement in his celebrated Nobel Prize winning poem, "The Wasteland." *Brhadaranyaka Upanishad* V.2.1-3.

devata – The effulgent. Hindus believe in many *devatas*. The *Rg Veda* is a collection of hymns addressed to many *devatas* – *Indra, Rudra, Varuna, Mitra, Agni, Vayu, Ushas, Pushan*, etc., the controllers of many natural phenomenon, like sacrificial fire, war and cattle, water, eyesight, fire, air, dawn, health and herbs, etc. In the *Puranas* we find *Vishnu, Shiva, Brahma, Ganesa, Skanda, Saraswati, Lakshmi, Durga, Krishna* and *Rama* replace these *devatas*. The religious seeker receives initiation from a *guru* in the form of a *mantra* with a *devata* to meditate upon who will be his or her guide.

devi – The female form of a *devata*, or a *deva*.

dharana – The practice of focusing the mind on a chosen object, deity or sound without distractions or dissimilar thoughts. The sixth step in yogic discipline. *Yoga Sutras* III.3. (See Patanjali; also *cittasya desa bandhata*)

dharmamegha samadhi – Spiritual absorption invoking a shower of bliss as a result of practicing Patanjali's eight-fold path of *yoga*. *Yoga Sutras* IV.28.

dhyana – A stage of meditation characterized by unbroken concentration on a chosen subject, deity or a sound without distracting, dissimilar thoughts; also a gesture assumed during meditation to invoke a certain state of consciousness. *Yoga Sutras* III.4. (See *mudra*; Patanjali)

diksha mantra – The *mantra* – syllables, words, phrases and/or sentences – given to a seeker by a *guru* at the time of initiation into a programme of spiritual discipline. The seeker meditates upon and repeats the *mantra* for gaining inner purity and concentration.

"*Divi surya sahasrasya bhasas tasya mahatmanah*" – Brilliance of that fully manifested universal form of the Lord; the experience when *kundalini* awakens and joins with the *sahasrara*, which can be compared to a thousand suns simultaneously arising. *Bhagavad Gita* XI.12.

Ganapatya – Followers of the tradition and worship of *Ganapathy*, the elephant-headed god of auspicious beginnings; son of *Siva* and *Parvathi*. No ritual begins in India without first propitiating *Ganapathy*.

Ganesa – Another name for the deity, *Ganapathy*, a popular deity in the Hindu pantheon.

Gayatri chandas – The metre in which the *Gayatri mantra* is composed which uses eight syllables per line.

Gayatri devata – The Lord Sun, worshipped in the female form and invoked by Hindu students with the chanting of the *Gayatri mantra*. (See *Gayatri mantra*)

Gayatri mantra – The *mantra* from the *Rg Veda* that has been chanted by millions of Hindu students down the centuries to attain memory power and a bright intellect. *Rg Veda* III.62.10.

gopuram – The front facade of a temple, especially South Indian temples, rising several hundred feet. The most famous *gopuram* is of the Goddess Temple of *Meenakshi* in Madurai, a south Indian city in Tamil Nadu.

gunatita – One who is beyond the play of the three *gunas* – *tamas, rajas* and *sattva* – the principles of inertia, activity, and knowledge, and who has come to identify with *Brahman*, the Universal Consciousness. *Bhagavad Gita* XIV.20.21.

guru – A spiritual preceptor; adept in scriptures, traditions, religious disciplines, who is spiritually realized. *Vivekachoodamani* 34-36. (See *siddha guru*) *guruvayu* – Literally, "exalted air" – that is, the breath because of which life is possible. (See *mukhyaprana*)

Hanumanji – Monkey god; the minister of Sugriva, the monkey king of Kiskinda; son of the wind god; servant of Lord Rama; the great scholar and military genius, herbalist, musician, life-long celibate; one of the heroes of the *Ramayana*, worshipped by millions of Hindus in temples and homes. The *Hanuman Chalisa* is a Hindi composition on Hanuman that is read daily by millions of Hindus seeking a long life, health, strength, a brilliant mind, success or freedom from enemies.

Himalayas – The great snowy mountain ranges spanning from *Hindu Kush*, the *Karakoram* mountain range in the northwest of the Indian subcontinent, to the mountains in Burma. The great Indian rivers – *Sindhu, Ganges, Brahmaputra* and the *Jamuna* – originate from the *Himalayas.* The loftiest mountain peaks – *Everest, Gaurisankar, Nandadevi* – are all included in these ranges. Considered holy by Hindus and a setting of Indian mythology, it is believed that all the souls of holy men reside there. Religious seekers leave everything and go to the *Himalayas. Himalaya* means the "abode of snow."

iccha sakti – One of the powers of *maya*; the supreme power of *Brahman* (the ultimate Reality in Hinduism); power of desire or will power. (See *sakti*)

indriya – Literally means "that which illumines" and refers to the sense organs, the organs of action, and the mind.

isvara – The power of *Brahman* manifested through *maya* (the dynamics of the three energies of the *gunas*); the Great Creator, Controller, and Constrictor.

isvarapranidhanam – Total surrender to God. An attitude Patanjali recommends for *yoga* practitioners. *Yoga Sutras* II.32.

jada dhyana – Absorption or concentration which is impermanent and, although one does not act in this state as one does when engaged in worldly activities, one still remains without the knowledge of the Truth or the Self. One can move in and out of this body-mind state.

jagat – That which appears and disappears, generally referring to the entire Creation.

jagat janani – The literal meaning is "Universal Mother." As Creatrix of the world, *Maya Sakti* is considered to be the active principle of creation or Mother of the Universe. According to the *Agama/Tantra Sastra*, *Siva* (or *Brahman*) is only a passive principle or witness.

jalatattva – The element of water situated in the *svadhisthan*, the sex centre. (See *cakra*)

jantu – *jayate mriyate iti jantu* – A definition of creatures from the standpoint of the perishable body – "that which is born and dies."

jiva – Consciousness or *Atman* reflected in the body-mind complex. It refers to the ego/doer/enjoyer who travels to lower or higher worlds as a result of individual thoughts and deeds. *Bhagavad Gita* XV.7-8.

jivabrahmaikya – Denotes the unity of the individual self with the Universal Self; that manifest plurality having its locus in the pure, limitless Consciousness. According to Sankaracharya, the foremost exponent of Advaita Vedanta, this vision is revealed in the *Upanishads*, the *Bhagavad Gita*, and the *Brahmasutras*.

jivatman – The same as *jiva*.

jnana – Knowledge, wisdom, enlightenment, Self-realization. As a posture, or *mudra*, it is sitting cross-legged with both hands resting on the knees, the index finger touching the tip of the thumb and the other three fingers held straight. It signifies unity of the *jivatman* (index finger) with *paramatman* (the thumb). This posture also produces neuropeptides and hormones resulting in inner quietude. (See *mudra*)

jnana sakti – The power of *Brahman* expressing through the *sattvic* aspect of *maya*, becomes *jnana sakti* omniscience, having the power of knowing all. (See *sakti*)

jyoti – Light – hence, light of knowledge; also spiritual light.

kama, kroda, lobha – Lust, anger, greed – three doors to hell and suffering. *Bhagavad Gita* XVI.21.

kaumara – Those who follow the worship of *Kumara* or *Skanda*, the second son of *Siva-Parvathi*. Although he is ever a teen-ager, he is also the general of the divine armies and a great teacher of spiritual knowledge. He wears only a loincloth. A lance is his weapon and a peacock his vehicle. Worshipped more in Tamil Nadu, a south Indian State. This deity's main temple is located in the foothills of the Western ghats at *Pazhani*.

Kerala – The southwestern state of India that had the world's first democratically-elected communist government. The state is noted for its full literacy, zero population growth, low industrialization, higher ratio of females in the population, and as the birthplace of Sankaracharya – the founder of Advaita Vedanta. Kerala means the land of *kera* or coconut.

kriya sakti – The power of *Brahman* expressing through *rajasic* aspect of *maya*. The power of doing and accomplishing. (See *sakti*)

Kumara – A Hindu god. (See *kaumara*)

kundala – Coiled. *Kundalam* is the noun form meaning a coil.

kundalini – The power of *maya*, as supreme power of *Brahman*, lying coiled in the lower *cakra* of the *jivatman*, at the *muladhara*. Upon awakening, one attains universal vision and unparalleled power.

laddu – An Indian sweet usually made at festival time and used as an offering to the deity. *Laddus* are also exchanged as gifts on special occasions.

Maharshi Mahesh Yogi – Founder of Transcendental Meditation, or TM, who has a worldwide following. His movement popularized Indian wisdom-traditions in the West including *ayurveda* and astrology.

Mahatma Gandhi – Mohan Das Karam Chand Gandhi, 1869-1948, the father of the modern Indian nation, who successfully led India's non-violent struggle against British colonization and became a martyr for Hindu-Muslim unity at the hands of a Hindu zealot. *Mahatma* means "great soul" and was the title given to Gandhi by Rabindra Nath Tagore, India's great poet, and subsequently has been adopted when referring to Gandhi.

manah – The feeling aspect of the mind. In the Indian spiritual tradition, purity of feeling and thought, or *sattva suddhi*, is an important prerequisite for seekers. (See *antahkarana*)

Manasarovar – The holy lake located at the foot of Mount Kailash, in Tibet, which is the abode of *Siva*. It symbolizes the pool of mind purified by austerities and devotional service.

manipura – The third *cakra* situated at the navel. (See *cakra*)

mantra – Syllables, sounds, utterances, sentences and verses used as spiritual energizers. (See *diksha mantra*)

mata – Denomination or form of worship. (See *shadmata sampradaya*)

maya sakti – The instrument of expressing *Brahman's* power and intent; constituted of *sattva, rajas, tamas* – the principles of knowledge, action and will.

mayaya pururupamiyade – The Vedic concept of one power appearing to be many by its inner dynamism (*mayaya*). *Pururupam* means many forms.

Mount Kailasa – The Hindu holy mountain, supposed to be

the abode of Lord Siva, the spiritual destination of seekers of *Siva*. Geographically located in Tibet.

mudra – A gesture or posture which reveals an inner state of mind, or when deliberately assumed, produces that desired state. *Sukha*, *bhakti*, *saranagati*, *prapatti*, *jnana*, *dhyana*, *yoga*, *bodha*, *prasada*, and *ananda* refer to specific *mudras* explained in the body of the text. (See the diagrams of these *mudras* in Chapter 2 and the Appendix.)

mukhyaprana – That breath which is primary to and controlling the five physiological functions and, consequently, all other physiological activities. (See *guruvayu*)

muladhara – (See *cakra*)

nadi – Subtle channels in the body carrying life energy, a million times thinner than the human hair.

Nambudri – Refers to Kerala *Brahmins* who are the custodians of the *Rg Veda* and the *Agnihotra* ritual. They are considered to be wise and live a simple life of austerity, secluded from the surrounding community. As landlords with massive holdings, they have a general contempt for physical labour. In Kerala, they often become the brunt of many jokes.

Narayana Guru – One of the greatest spiritual masters of Kerala who lived from 1854-1928. He was a lower caste Hindu and a realized Vedantin who wrote prolifically. The lower caste community to which *Narayana Guru* belonged became known as "toddy tappers" as this caste customarily extracted the sap from coconut and palm trees to make liquor. *Narayana Guru* was responsible for a movement against liquor consumption. He also organized a movement for promoting mass education on a platform that emphasized organization, industrialization and the unity of religions.

"Nasadasid nosadasid tadanim" – The famous *Rg Veda* hymn, *Nsasadiya Sukta*, which reflects on timelessness – "In the beginning there was neither aught nor naught." *Rg Veda* X.129.

nididhyasana – The third step in Vedantic discipline. After listening to the scriptures and reflecting upon their inner meaning, the seeker is asked to practice *nididhyasana*, repeated meditation on the Truth as unitive consciousness.

nirbija – The culminating stage in *samadhi* in which all tendencies and seeds of the ego are finally destroyed. Total Self-realization; Self-rootedness; the "I am That" *Soham* cognition without the taint of past tendencies (the ego). *Yoga Sutras* I.51. (See *samadhi*)

nirbijasahaja samadhi – That state of effortless, seedless, non-returning Self-Abidance.

nirvicara – A stage in *samadhi* in which quite effortless witnessing of all thought modifications happens. There are three thought-modifications -- pleasant, agitated and dull – that occur due to the play of the *gunas* and are conditioned by habits. *Yoga Sutras* I.44. (See *samadhi*)

nirvitarka – Steadiness in the knowledge of the changeable nature of the world and the resultant natural and effortless detachment from worldly objects. Effortless seeing of the world as devoid of content and as an ever-changing flux. *Yoga Sutras* I.43. (See *samadhi*)

niyama – The five-fold personal disciplines Patanjali prescribed for a *yoga* practitioner – purity, cheerfulness, austerity or the observance of discipline, self-study and surrender to God. *Yoga Sutras* II.32. (See *yama*)

Om Nama Shivaya – "I offer myself unto *Siva*;" a salutation to Lord Shiva. A *mantra* a novice chants for attaining mental purity and concentration by means of reducing desires and inner tensions. (See: *mantra*)

osadibhyonnam – "Food is modification of herbs and plants." *Taittiriya Upanisad* II.1.

padmasana – The lotus posture; one of the prescribed postures for *yoga* practitioners.

pancabhutas – The five primary elements born of the three-fold *maya*. They are: space (*akasa*), air (*vayu*), fire (*agni*), water (*apah*), and earth (*prthvi*). The entire universe is put together from these five elements and their compounds. (See *Tattva Bodha* of Sankaracharya and *Vedanta Sara* of Sadananda.)

Patanjali – The great exponent of the Hindu psycho-physical discipline of *yoga* for spiritual unfoldment. His period of existence is unknown but is estimated to be at least 5000 years ago.

prana – The breath is meditated upon as visible God in *yoga* practice. The concept of *prana* is further explained by this quotation: "*Namaste, Vayo tvameva pratyaksam Brahmasi, tvameva pratyaksam Brahma vadisyami*:" "Salutations to you, Air; you indeed are the visible God; I assert that my breath is indeed manifest *Brahman*." (*Krishna Yajurveda*, Peace Invocation)

pranava – Literally, "salutations." The sound "*Om*" by which one salutes the Lord, and hence *Om* is known as the *pranava*. *Om* is also the name of the Lord. *Yoga Sutras* I.27.

pranayama – Regulated, conscious breathing coupled with chanting of *Om* for purifying spiritual channels and awakening the *kundalini* and experiencing *Brahman*. The four steps in the practice of *pranayama* are: *puraka, antakumbhaka, recaka,* and, *bahyakumbhaka*. *Puraka* is to inhale either with one nostril blocked or through both nostrils – a slow, steady and deep inhaling to fill the lungs. *Antakumbhaka* involves the retention of the breath inside, four times more than it took to breathe in. *Recaka* is exhaling – the slow, steady and total exhalation of breath through one nostril or through both, doubling the time it took to breathe in. Finally, *bahyakumbhaka*, the last step in *pranayama* practice, involves the pause before again inhaling or, in other words, keeping the lungs devoid of breath. This phase is to be maintained double the time of inner retention. *Yoga Sutras* II.29; 49.

prani – It means, "one who breathes." The concept of *prani* is further explained by this quotation: "*prana yasya asti iti – prani*;" the human being is called a *prani*, as "one who breathes is called a *prani*."

prapatti – Unconditional surrender to God. The *prapatti mudra* creates this attitude. (See *mudra*)

prasada – *Prasada mudra* is the expression of an attitude of acceptance of inevitable happenings in life. *Prasada* is that which is sanctified through offering. (See *mudra*)

pratyahara – Detached or withdrawn state of mind in *yoga*. *Yoga Sutras* I.52. (See *Patanjali*)

prthviyam osadhayah – Herbs and plants are grown in earth and, hence, a modification of earth. *Taittiriya Upanishad* II.1.

puraka, purakam – (See *pranayama*) *Purakam* is the noun form.

rajas – One aspect of the triadic energies of *maya*, the mysterious power of *Brahman*. *Rajas* is the dynamic, active, evolutionary aspect of *maya*. (See *triguna*)

raksasa – One who employs any means to achieve his ambitions and goals; a ruthless, reckless, sensuous and materialistic person.

Rama – Lord Rama, an incarnation of *Vishnu*, son of King Dasaratha of Ayodhya, the hero of the *Ramayana*. Millions of Hindus worship Lord Rama as virtue incarnate. He fought and won a bloody war with Ravana, his archenemy, who abducted his wife Sita.

Ramana Maharshi – The sage of *Arunachala*, a mountain shrine of the South Indian state, Tamil Nadu. After his near-death experience at the age of 16, he came to *Arunachala* Hill and spent the rest of his life in silent communion with his infinite blissful Self. He was great teacher whose spiritual method consisted of inquiry into the "I." (1879-1950 A. D.)

Ramayana – The great epic of Hindus, authored by sage Valmiki. The *Ramayana*, or the *Life of Rama*, has 26,000 verses in simple couplets.

recaka, recakam – (See *pranayama*)

rishi – Refers to a *Vedic* seer, like Vasista and Visvamitra.

rudraksa mala – Necklace of *rudraksa* beads used for chanting *mantras*, famous for medicinal properties.

sabija – Literally, "with seeds." In connection with *samadhi* it means "Self-abidance with seeds" or absorption with remnants of old egoistic tendencies still operative in the psyche which may sprout at unguarded moments. Self-realization or *Soham*-cognition, but without totally overcoming old tendencies. *Yoga Sutras* I.46. (See *samadhi*)

"Sadeva idam agre asid" – "Only one homogenous Truth was there in the beginning." *Chandogya Upanishad* VI.2.1.

sadhaka – One who practices a programme of spiritual discipline under the guidance of a *guru* who follows a tradition.

sadhana – The rigorous disciplines prescribed for a spiritual seeker.

sahaja – A natural effortless state of boundless, blissful Consciousness. Total egolessness, timelessness and divisionlessness. (See *samadhi*)

sahasrara – The seventh *cakra* in the *kundalini vidya* described as the seat of Supreme Bliss, situated in and surrounding the brain, where a million lotuses of spiritual ecstasy bloom.

sajatiya vrtti pravaham – The unbroken flow of similar thoughts; the definition of *dhyana* or concentration. *Yoga Sutras* III.2.

saksibhava – State of witnessing thought and sensations without indulgence, resistance, judgment or attachment.

sakteyas – Worshippers of *Sakti, Kali* and *Durga*; the female principle of the Godhead.

sakti – The Cosmic Power adored in the form of the Universal Mother and invoked for guidance by a novice. Along with *Siva* and *Vishnu, Sakti* is an important deity in the Hindu pantheon. A symbol of power and compassion, she relentlessly fights against the forces of evil. In Vedanta, *sakti* is a power dependent upon *Brahman*, the Supreme invisible Truth, whereas in popular worship, *sakti* is considered a co-equal power with *Siva*. (See *iccha sakti*, *kriya sakti*, and *jnana sakti*).

"*Saktiman: sakti yasya asti iti*" – "God, who enjoys infinite power in the form of knowledge, will and action;" *Brahman's* creative phase.

samadhi – Equal vision; motiveless compassion; total egolessness; steady mindedness; Self-abidance, spiritual bliss; dis-identification with the ego-mind-body complex; living in God-Consciousness. (See Patanjali: *savitarka*; *nirvitarka*; *savicara*; *nirvicara*; *samprajnata*; *asamprajnata*; *sabija*; *nirbija*; and, *sahaja*. For further discussion of these terms: *antara sabdanuviddha*; *bahya sabdanuviddha*; *antara drisyanuviddha*; *bahya drsyanuviddha*, see *Drgdrsyaviveka* 23-25).

samasti prana – The vital air which animates all living beings. The life-force that courses through the veins of the universal person.

samprajnata – The state of absorption in *samadhi* with the consciousness of duality of "I and my bliss." A deliberate watching of thoughts and sensations, identifying with the light of Consciousness. *Yoga Sutras* I.17.

samyas – See *sanyas*.

Sanatana dharma – The views and way of life expounded in the Vedas; a life based on truth and non-violence; the eternal universal law of existence. In contemporary Hinduism, *Sanatana dharma* includes Veda, Vedanta, Pauranic (mythological) teachings and image worship along with rituals. By contrast, *Arya Samaja dharma* rejects image worship and mythology.

Sankara – Sankaracharya, the great exponent of Advaita Vedanta, seer and scholar, who lived from 788-820 A. D. He wrote commentaries on Hindu scriptures, established *maths* (monasteries), banished Buddhism from India, and re-established the *Vedic-Brahmanic* religion of modern Hinduism.

Sanyas (samnyas) – Renunciation of doer-ship in interactions and activities; renouncing possessiveness; renouncing limitations in the light of Self-knowledge.

sanyasi – A renunciant; one who is established in the Self; a wandering ascetic; one who is fearless and causes fear to none; one who does work without either ego or desire for personal reward; one who is ever happy.

Sanskrit – An ancient language written in *Devanagari* script and perfected by the *astadhyayi* grammar of Panini. The Vedas, Puranas, and all ancient Hindu literature on art, science, philosophy and religion are written in Sanskrit. It is no longer a spoken language in India, but lives on in all modern Indian languages.

santosam – Bliss.

saranagati – Surrender to the Lord. (See *mudra*)

sarira – The three bodies – gross, subtle, causal – all perishable and ever-changing.

"*Sarvarambha hi dosena dhumenagnir ivavrta*" – "All beginnings and/or activities are clouded by defects as is fire by smoke." *Bhagavad Gita* XVIII.48.

sastra – Hindu scriptures containing spiritual and moral instructions.

Sat – The Truth; Brahman; the Changeless.

sattva – One of the energies of *maya,* the energy of light, cognition, and purity. (See *triguna*)

sattvatita – Beyond *sattva,* the enlightened one who is not controlled by the play of the *gunas.* (See *gunatita*)

sattvic – That which enjoys, or is born of, or is a modification of *sattva.*

satyam – Same as *Sat*: Truth, *Brahman,* the Changeless.

saucam – Cleanliness, purity.

saureya – One who follows the worship of *Surya,* the Sun god.

savicara – The effort to watch and detach from the ever-changing flux of inner thoughts. Watching (*vicara*) inner thought modifications that manifest due to past impressions and habits. *Yoga Sutras.* I.44. (See *samadhi*)

savitarka – Effort to see the hollowness of the ever-changing world of matter and sense experiences. Not seeking joy in worldly possessions and achievements and coming to realize the changeable nature of the world – all by a process of *tarka,* or logical understanding, with the help of the scriptures. *Yoga Sutras* I.42. (See *samadhi*)

shadmata sampradaya – The six deities and their traditional rituals of worship, including meditation. Established by Sankaracharya from a medley of Hindu deities. The six deities are *Surya*, *Ganesa*, *Kumara* (*Skanda*), *Vishnu*, *Sakti*, and *Siva*.

Shaivas – Devotees of *Siva*, a Hindu deity.

Siva – One of the three important Hindu gods. Devotees of *Siva* consider Him to be the Supreme Godhead. His abode is Mount Kailasa and his consort is *Parvathi*. His vehicle is *Nandi*, the bull. He is draped in a tiger skin. *Vasuki*, the king of snakes curls around his neck. His forehead is besmeared with holy ashes, and a crescent moon adorns the matted locks of hair where *Ganga*, his secret love, hides. He is also called "the three-eyed." (See *Shaivas*)

Siva-Sakti tandava – The experience of bliss as the *kundalini* arises and reaches *Siva* in the *sahasrara cakra* of a *yogi*; as this energy breaks out, all ego limitations dissolve and the *yogi* enjoys limitless bliss – the dance of *Siva-Sakti* – in an eternal, all-consuming embrace. Also called *Siva-Saktisamyoga*.

Shivoham – "I am *Siva*," the infinite consciousness. A *mantra* repeated by an advanced aspirant. (See *mantra*)

siddha guru – One who is the God-Realized Self. One who has studied, practiced, meditated and realized God-hood, Truth, Joy and Bliss.

sloka – Sanskrit verse.

Soham – "I am He." A *mantra* used to become established in the unitive experience

sthambhana – Retention of the breath. (See *pranayama*)

sthirasukhamasanam – (See *asana*)

stotram – A hymn adoring a deity.

Sugriva – The monkey king of Kishkinda in South India of *Ramayana* times, who along with his minister, Hanuman, served Rama in retrieving Sita from the island of Sri Lanka.

sukha – Pleasant, happy. (See *mudra*)

sukhasana – Refers to the *mudra* or posture which invokes peace and happiness. A comfortable posture that provides a maximum base to the body. The legs are folded with the hands resting upon the knees. This posture is easier than the lotus posture. (See *asana*)

suksma buddhi – A subtle intellect, purified by study, service and austerities.

Surya – The Sun god. (See *saureya*)

suryadevata – The *devata,* deity or celestial being of the Sun.

susumna – The invisible channel along the vertebral column linking *kundalini* and the *cakras*, from the *muladhara* to the *sahasrara*. An adept uses this channel for uniting his energy with cosmic intelligence. (See *cakra*)

sutra – Aphoristic sentences. A form of writing different from Vedic *mantras* and *Pauranic slokas.* The six Hindu systems of philosophy are written in *sutra* form. *Sutra* means "a thread" which is typically used to string together flowers or beads, but in this case, it refers to the threading together of philosophical ideas. (See *Yoga Sutras*)

svadhisthan – The second psychic centre situated at the root of the sex organ. (See *cakra*)

svarita – Modulation of the pitch in chanting a *mantra*.

"*Svarupa sunyam iva arthamatra nirbhasa*" – "Cognition of Truth without the corrupting limitations of ego and memory." The state of *samadhi*. *Yoga Sutras* I.43.

"*Tada drastuh svarupe avasthanam*" – "Then, when mind is quiet, abidance in the true nature of the seer *of* the mind happens." *Yoga Sutras* I.3.

Taittiriya Upanishad – One of the ten major *Upanishads* having Sankaracharya's commentary; it belongs to the *Krishna Yajurveda*.

tamas – One mode of energy of *maya* characterized by inertia, darkness, and obstinacy. (See *triguna*)

tamasic – Having a predominance of the *tamas*.

tapa – Austerities and disciplines. *Yoga Sutras* II.1; 31; *Bhagavad Gita* XVII.14-16.

tiksna buddhi – A sharp intellect, trained in material science and in the ways of the world. (See *buddhi*)

trataka – Concentration on the point between the eyebrows or at the root of the tongue.

triguna – The three energies of *maya*. (See *tamas, rajas, sattva*)

Trisanku – One who has lost his way, neither here nor there, or who is in a deep dilemma; one who has lost his purpose in life, is indecisive and confused. This story illustrates the point: *Indra*, the King of gods, refuses permission to Trisanku to enter heaven. Visvamitra – the royal sage who had his own score to settle with *Indra* – was approached by Trisanku. Visvamitra made a new heaven for Trisanku and sent him there. But that heaven never flourished, and although Trisanku was totally unhappy, he could not annoy Visvamitra by leaving the semi-built heaven. Hence, he was in the utmost dilemma.

"*Trividham narakasyedam dvaram*" – "These are the three gates to hell – lust, anger and greed." *Bhagavad Gita* XVI.21.

tulsi mala – A garland made of *tulsi* (basil) beads used by *Vaisnavas* for counting as they recite *mantras*. The beads are made from the stem of the plant. The *tulsi* is famous for its medicinal properties.

udata – Modulation of the pitch in chanting a *mantra*.

Universal Mother – *Maya* worshipped as the all-compassionate, all-powerful image of the Cosmic Mother by followers of *Säkti*.

Upanishad – Literally, to "sit down near" or to "live near." Refers to the later portion of the Vedas dealing with meditation and knowledge of the Self. There are thirteen main *Upanishads*, of which ten have commentaries written by Sankaracharya.

upasaka – One who practises *upasana*.

upasana – A meditation on a chosen deity; chanting of *mantras*; observing silence; fasting.

upasyadevata – One's chosen deity for guidance and meditation.

upasyam – The object of *upasana*.

utsav – A celebration, especially one centred on a deity.

vaishnavas – Devotees of Lord *Vishnu*.

"*Vayo tvameva pratyaksam brahmasi, tvameva pratyaksam brahma vadisyami*" – "Salutations to you, Air; you indeed are the perceptible God; I assert that my breath is indeed manifest *Brahman*." (*Krishna Yajurveda, Taittiriya Upanishad,* Peace Invocation)

Veda – The four sacred Hindu scriptures: the *Rg Veda*, the *Yajur Veda*, *Sama Veda* and the *Atharva Veda*. They deal with spiritual, moral, ethical, psychological and physical subjects.

Vedanta – The "end" portion or culmination of the Vedas that deals with meditation, wisdom, and the Self.

Vedantin – One who ascribes to the Vedantic vision of the unity of existence underlying the world, God and the experiencing individual.

vibhuti – The holy ash that devotees of *Siva* use to smear on their forehead and other parts of the body. It also refers to the glories of *Siva*.

vicara – (See *savicara*)

Vishnu – One of the triad of Hindu deities. The protector of the universe. He is also called *Narayana*. He is generally envisaged in a reclining pose on a 1000-headed serpent that arches over him; his consort, *Lakshmi*, ever-massages his feet; the eagle, *Garuda*, King of birds, is his vehicle. *Vishnu* is advised by seven *rishis* and wields in his four hands the insignia of his glories – the discus, the mace, the conch and the lotus. (See *Vaishnavas*)

visuddha – The fifth *cakra* situated in the throat region. (See *cakra*)

vrttisajatyam dhyanam – A state of concentration which is indicated by similarity in successive thoughts.

Vyasa – The greatest of Hindu scholar-sages. The compiler of the four Vedas; author of the *Mahabharata*, the 18 *Puranas* and the *Brahmasutras*. The founder of Hinduism as we know it today. He was born of a physically lame *Brahmin* scholar and a young, dark fisher-woman who conceived Vyasa midstream in a boat. He grew up on an islet in the mighty Yamuna River of North India. His full name is Krishna Dwaipayana Parasara Badarayana Veda Vyasamuni. (See *Brahmasutras*)

yama – A set of five disciplines Patanjali prescribes for *yoga* practitioners: truthfulness, non-violence, continence, non-stealing, and non-possessiveness. *Yoga Sutras* II.30.

yoga – Union with Self; dissociation with non-self and dialogue with the inner self; work without expectation; psychic-physical disciplines; egoless awareness; path to God. Equanimity of mind; pursuit of excellence in work; rootedness in one's Self; love for all. (See *mudra*)

yogi – One who practices *yoga*.

Yoga Sutras – A compilation of 195 aphorisms on *yoga* discipline, its aim and results, by the sage Patanjali.

APPENDIX

Nanacchidraghadodarasthita maha

dipaprabha bhasvaram

Jnanam yasya tu caksuradikarana

dvara bahihspandate,

Janamiti tameva bhantamanubha –

tyetatsamastam jagat

Tasmai Sri Guru murtaye nama idam Sri Dakshinamurtaye.

(Hymn to Dakshinamurti, sloka 4)

Translation: Just as a lamp placed in a pot with holes in it shoots beams of light out and illuminates the objects in their paths, the light of Consciousness reflected in the mind as the, "I know; I know" experience shoots out through the sense organs – that is, the eyes, the ears, etc. – illuminating its respective objects – that is forms, sounds, etc. – and creates sensory experiences – that is "I see," "I hear," etc. I salute that light of Consciousness in the form of Sri Dakshinamurti, who is the ultimate guru.

Paranci khani vyatrnat svayambhuh

tasmat paran pasyati na antaratman

kaschit dhirah pratyagatmanam aikshat

Avrtta caksur amrtatvam icchan

(Kathopanisad, II.4.1)

Translation: The Creator created sense organs with an extroverted propensity; therefore, human beings see only external objects – alas, not the inner Self. A rare discerning one, desiring immortality, develops detachment and beholds the boundless Self.

Lokesmin dvividha nishta

pura prokta mayanagha

jnana yogena samkhyanam

karma yogena yoginam

(Bhagavad Gita, III.3)

Translation: In ancient times, O Sinless One, I taught that there were two paths in this world – the path of knowledge for those enjoying *viveka*, and the path of action (*karma yoga*), for those with likes and dislikes who want to achieve purity of mind.

ॐ

Samnyasas tu mahabaho

duhkham aptum ayogatah

yogayukto munir brahma

nacirenadhigacchati

(Bhagavad Gita, (V.6)

Translation: O Mighty-Armed One, renunciation of doership is difficult to attain for one who has not practiced *karma yoga*. Endowed with purity of mind (non-reaction in action), such a *muni* attains *Brahman* without delay.

Aruruksor muner yogam

karma karanam ucyate

yogarudhasya tasyaiva

samah karanam ucyate

(Bhagavad Gita, VI.3)

Translation: For that seeker who would mount *karma yoga*, it is said that activity is the means. For one who has succeeded in balancing an active mind, efforts for self-abidance (like *sravana*, *manana* and *nididhyasana*) are said to be the means.

Om Brahmavidapnoti param

tadeshabbhyuktah

satyam jnanamanantam brahma

yo veda nihitam guhayam parame vyoman

sosnute sarvan kaman saha

Brahmana vipasciteti

tasmadva etasmadatmana akasah sambhutah

akasadvayuh vayoragnih

agnerapah adbhya prthvi

prthviya osadhayah osadibhyonnam

annatpurusah

(Taittiriya Upanisad, II.1)

Translation: The knower of *Brahman* attains the Supreme Bliss. About that *Brahman* this is said: "*Brahman* is changeless, limitless Consciousness." He who realizes that *Brahman* in the pure space of his heart as his essential self, fulfills all his desires. From that *Brahman*, which is identical with the (self or) knower of *Brahman*, manifests the space element, from the space element manifest air; from that air element manifests fire; from that fire element manifests water; from that water element manifests earth; and from that earth element manifest herbs and plants, from which manifest food, from which manifest living beings.

Namaste vayo

tvameva pratyaksam brahmasi

tvameva pratyaksam brahma vadisyami

rtam vadisyami

satyam vadisyami

tanmamavatu tadvaktaramavatu

(Taittiriya Upanishad, Invocation)

Translation: Salutations to *Vayu*. You are no other than *Brahman*. I will declare that you are truly *Brahman* and righteousness itself. I will declare that you are Truth. May *Brahman*, as *Vayu*, protect me. May he protect the teacher.

Purnamada purnamidam

purnat purnamudacyate

purnasya purnamadaya

purnamevavasisyate

Aum Santih Santih Santih

(Brhadaranyaka & Isa Upanishad, Invocation)

Translation: That is whole; this is whole; from the whole, the whole becomes manifest. From the whole, when the whole is negated, again remains the whole.

Aum sarve bhavantu sukhinah

sarve santu niramayah

sarve bhadrani pasyantu

ma kaschit duhkhabhag bhavet

Aum Santih Santih Santih

(Ancient Sanskrit Prayer)

Translation: Om. May one and all be happy; may one and all be healthy. May all see what is auspicious. May none suffer. Peace be! Peace be! Peace be!

Aum asato ma sadgamaya

tamaso ma jyotirgamaya

mrtyorma amrtam gamaya

Aum Santih Santih Santih

(Brhadaranyaka Upanisad, I.3.28)

Translation: Lead us from untruth to Truth. Lead us from darkness to Light. Lead us from death to Immortality. Om, Peace! Peace! Peace!

Ten Mudras

1. Sukha Mudra

2. Jnana Mudra

3. Dhyana Mudra

4. Yoga Mudra

5. Bhakti Mudra

6. Saranagati Mudra

7. Prapatti Mudra

8. Bodha Mudra

9. Prasada Mudra

10. Ananda Mudra

ASHRAMS & ORGANIZATIONS

Swami Bodhananda, Founder & Spiritual Director

Sambodh Foundation

K-11 Kailash Colony
New Delhi, 110 048 India
Tel: (011) 2628 9247

Bodhananda Research Foundation
for Management& Leadership Studies
Bodhananda Kendra

Kalady, Karamana P.O.
Thiruvananthapuram 695 002
Tel: (0471) 344 084 / 433 084

Bodhananda Seva Society &
Bodhananda Kendra

Kalady, Karamana P.O.
Thiruvananthapuram 695 002
Tel: (0471) 344 084 / 433 084

Vrindavan Vanaprastha Ashram
for the Elderly
Bodhananda Kendra

Kalady, Karamana P.O.
Thiruvananthapuram 695 002
Tel: (0471) 344 084 / 433 084

Bodhananda Kendra

Kizhakkepattu, Chevarambalam P.O.
Kozhikode 673 017
Tel: (0495) 373 527 / 355 474

Bodhananda Kendra

Puliyathu Mukku, Kilikollur P.O.
Kollam 691 004
Tel: (0474) 718 905 / 719021

Ashraya Training Centre
A Residential School for Handicapped Girl Children

Puliyathu Mukku, Kilikollur P.O.
Kollam 691 004
Tel: (0474) 718 905 / 719 021

Sambodh Foundation

c/o S. Gopalakrishnan
G-190 Sahakara Nagara
Kodigehalli
Bangalore 560 092
Tel: (080) 353 5500

Bodhananda Sruti Seva Trust

Bhadra, 2/594, Vazhakkala, Trikkakara PO
Ernakulum, Cochin 682 021
Tel: (0484) 421 029 / 421 029

The Sambodh Society, Inc.

Dr. Ruth Harring, Ph.D., Trustee
USA Program Coordinator
1826 Charter Avenue
Kalamazoo, Michigan 49024
USA
Tel: (616) 327 3774
Email: Indiaink@worldnet.att.net

Dr. Uma Deperalta. M.D., Trustee

7002 N. La Presa Drive
San Gabriel, California 91775
USA
Tel: (269) 292 6883